Inside Jihad

Understanding and Confronting Radical Islam

By Dr. Tawfik Hamid

Copyright & Publisher Information

First edition: March 2008

ISBN: 978-0-9815471-0-7

Self published book.

Library of Congress Control Number: 2008900898

Table of Contents

Introduction

We are confronted today with the seemingly intractable scourge of Islamic Terrorism. Some experience it in-person, most encounter the spectacle of it on their television screens. Our minds are haunted by images of 9/11, of the Bali nightclubs, of subways in Madrid and London, and of schoolchildren in Beslan. We witness daily misery in myriad locations around the globe. Jihadists behead innocent people on videotape, and billions watch it.

It has led decent people to ask questions and seek answers: "What kind of person could do this?", "What is the purpose?", "What caused this and who is to blame?" Naturally, we also ask, "What can we do about it?" Today, countless books are available about Islam and Islamic terror, and we do read them. Not long ago words like "Sharia" and "Wahabbi" would have met with blank stares from acquaintances. Now, while many readers are familiar with these terms, there still remains profound confusion about Islamism. A large percentage of non-Muslims continue to be mystified by an ideological cancer on the body of approximately 1.5 billion Islamic adherents.

Critics have leveled the charge at me that I am anti-Islam. Nothing is farther from the truth. I am in fact a Muslim and I consider much in Islam to be beautiful and worthwhile. However, the way it is taught today in most communities is perverted and destructive. Radical Islam could only have arisen in a community that prepared the ground for its evil seeds to sprout. I am convinced, therefore, that Islam is in need of reformation, or extensive re-interpretation, and that such change is entirely possible. To this end I have worked extensively, and in the final chapter I outline the key elements of Islamic reformation.

The 20th century bestowed upon us the carnage of the World Wars, Nazi concentration camps and Soviet labor camps. It has borne witness to genocide in places as disparate as

Cambodia, Rwanda, and Bosnia. If we have gained anything from that experience, we would expect it to be the capacity to diagnose ideological and societal illnesses, to confront them and defeat them. Sadly, that expectation leads to disappointment. Recent events in Darfur testify to a spotty record of inaction, indifference, and misdirected blame, of ignorance and feigned ignorance.

So too is it the case with jihad. I hope, in writing this book, to employ my personal experience to clarify the problem of Islamic terrorism and to propose workable approaches to neutralize it. I am certainly familiar with the time constraints of most readers – television, books, radio, and newspapers compete with the new media of blogs, email and instant messages to monopolize our spare moments as never before. I have therefore chosen to keep this book to a reasonable length, so that even the busiest members of our society may read it.

Note: I intentionally did not use traditional translations of the Quran as many of them do not convey the exact understanding of the verse. For this reason, I translated the Quranic verses from Arabic (my mother tongue) into English in a way to convey how the verse is understood and interpreted by most Islamic scholars.

Tawfik Hamid
28 January 2008

A Brief Overview of Islam

This is not a book about Islam – it is a book about Islamism and how to combat it. We cannot confront the problem of Islamism, however, without a general mental picture of Islam. The reader will encounter various Arabic words and Islamic concepts and must have some familiarity with them if any discussion about the topic is to make sense. That is what these next few pages undertake. They are not a substitute for a complete and detailed exposition of the religion. That role is played by the many excellent books devoted to the subject, and to which the reader is encouraged to turn. Indeed, many commonly-available encyclopedias provide an adequate coverage of Islam if a reader lacks the time or inclination to examine a complete treatise. In turn, some readers may already be knowledgeable about Islam; they may safely skip this overview. Here, I will cover only the main structural components of the religion and corresponding terms which are critical to our discussion. With these constraints in mind, let us introduce Islam.

The word Islam means "submission" to God, or Allah. It is a monotheistic faith that originated in the 7th century with its prophet, Muhammad. The primary text is the Quran, which Muslims believe is the literal word of God transmitted to the Prophet by the angel Gabriel. The revelation of the Quran to Muhammad is marked by Islam's holiest month, *Ramadan*. Muhammad was born in the Arabian Peninsula, an area holy to Muslims, who call it, in Arabic, the *hijaz*. The region encompasses the holy cities of Mecca and Medina. These cities are visited every year by millions of Muslims as part of their obligatory pilgrimage, known as the *haj*.

Initially, Prophet Muhammad faced persecution for his new faith. As time passed, he was able to gather adherents and control the city of Medina, where he established his authority. From there, he fought battles against the armies of Mecca with mixed results. Eventually, by employing a strategy of constriction and direct assault, Muhammad overcame the city with little struggle. During that time, a quarrel arose between the Jews of Medina and Muhammad's followers, which led to the quick destruction of the Jewish community. This destruction, in combination with further conversion and conquest, enabled Muhammad to consolidate power. By the time of his death in 632, Muhammad ruled the entire *hijaz*. After his death, Muslims selected a prince, or *caliph*, to lead an Islamic government called the Caliphate. Historians distinguish between several caliphates. They were headquartered in various cities and were the source of some internal conflict, including that between Sunni and Shia which we still see today. However, under the first caliphs – and remarkably, in less than 150 years – Islam had exploded across the Middle East, North Africa, and parts of Europe in what is known as the Islamic Conquest. In a short span of time, many native languages and religions disappeared; they were swallowed-up by the Arabic language and Islam.

Because he was the final prophet, chosen to reveal God's last message, and also because of his success, most Muslims consider the *Sunna* – or words and deeds of Muhammad – to be a foundational component of Islam. These exploits of Muhammad are recorded in chronicles known as hadith, a word employed in both the singular and plural sense (although "*hadiths*" is popular among English speakers).

The Quran itself is divided into 114 chapters, called *suwar* (more commonly referred to in the singular, *sura*, and in the anglicized plural, "suras"), which contain a total of 6236 poetic verses, or *ayat*. The word of God was revealed to Muhammad not at once, but over a period of time. Therefore, earlier suras typically concern themselves with spiritual and ethical matters, while later suras are preoccupied with regulation of society, for example, marital relations, criminal punishment, and war.[1] The Quran cannot cover every aspect

---

[1]Interestingly, the suras are not necessarily arranged chronologically; lower-numbered suras were sometimes written later. For example, Sura 2 was written during the Medina period (late stages of revelation), while Sura 114 – the last Sura in the Quran – was written in the very early stages of Islam, in the Mecca period. Thus, when we speak of "earlier suras" we mean earlier in time, not "earlier" in number.

of Islamic life, so many Muslims look to the *Sunna* (as recorded in the hadiths) for guidance when the Quran is silent.

The hadiths comprised a very large body of oral tradition, propagated and built upon for hundreds of years, until at last they were assembled and recorded under the Abbasid Caliphate. At that time, it was discovered that many *hadith* were contradictory or dubious, so efforts were made to classify them in terms of their accuracy, and by extension, importance. The term for "accurate" is *sahih*, and the two collections of hadiths considered most accurate and which are most renowned are *Sahih al-Buchary* and *Sahih Muslim*. The former was written before 870 CE by Imam Buchary and contains 7275 hadiths; the latter before 875 by Muslim and contains 9200 hadiths.

Although Islam has a number of sects and systems of belief, Muslims typically are required to obey the so-called "Five Pillars of Islam". The first pillar, called *shahada*, is the basic testament of every Muslim: "I testify that there is none worthy of worship except God and I testify that Muhammad is the Messenger of God." The testament is uttered upon conversion to Islam, and any Muslim who disputes it is considered an apostate. Islam does not practice baptism as Christianity does, nor does it have any other important initiation ritual.

The second pillar, *salah*, is the obligation to pray, typically five times per day. Notably, the Quran says nothing about the prayers being five, merely:

> *And establish regular prayers at the two ends of the day and at the approaches of the night: For those things, that are good remove those that are evil: Be that the word of remembrance to those who remember (their Lord)*
> {Quran 11:114}

The injunction to pray five times per day, as opposed to another number, is derived from the hadiths. Indeed, some sects pray three times per day, while some Sufi Muslims do not believe that ritualistic prayer is even necessary.

The third pillar, *zakah*, is that of charity. It is very similar to the Christian concept of the tithe. Every Muslim is required to assist less fortunate Muslims, based on his or her capacity to do so. There are various subsidiary types of *zakah*, the details of which are not important to our discussion.

Fourth is the pillar called *sawm*, which means "to fast". Fasts are typically performed for repentance, as part of a ritual, or to commune with God. Muslims are required to fast during the month of Ramadan.

Finally, we have already mentioned the fifth pillar of Islam: the *haj*. Once in every Muslim's life he or she is required to journey to Mecca and worship, if circumstances permit. The *haj* takes up the entire Islamic month of Dhu al-Hijjah.

It is surprising to some that the concept of Five Pillars is never mentioned clearly in the Quran. The notion is based on a well-known saying of Prophet Muhammad. Nevertheless, it is a core, and for many, the most familiar component of Islam.

Finally, Islamic Law, or *Sharia*, is central to Islamic life today. Sharia has a long and extensive tradition. It is a both a legal system and code of conduct that covers a vast array of issues, from criminal law to government matters to problems of daily life. It concerns itself with marriage, punishments, inheritance, and banking; with worship, charity, and civil cases. Scholars of Sharia, known as *ulema*, are responsible for interpreting Sharia and applying it to new situations. Sharia takes for its basis the Quran, the *Sunna*, the actions of Muhammad's disciples, the *fiqh* (or jurisprudence), and various *tafseer* (explanations) of the Quran. Sharia is considered by Muslims to be Divine Law, and more importantly, is considered by many to be the only Law that should, ultimately, be respected. Sharia, therefore, plays a critical role in Islamism – as we will soon discover.

Chapter 1:

The Making of an Islamic Terrorist

Chapter 1: The Making of an Islamic Terrorist

Childhood

Islamism didn't find very fruitful ground in Egypt under President Gamal Abdel Nasser – it didn't fit into his secular ideology of pan-Arab socialism. Nasser aligned himself with the Soviets, accepting their military aid and advisors. Although he was a sworn enemy of the United States, Nasser saw militant Islam as the larger menace. During the period when he held power (1956-1970), he cracked down on Islamist incitement and violence.[2] Travel to and from traditionally Islamic nations, such as Saudi Arabia, was strictly curtailed because he feared their Wahabbi sect would propagate a militant brand of Islam known as Salafism.

It was at the time of his regime that I was born, in 1961, to a secular Muslim family in Cairo. My mother was a French teacher whose political views were generally liberal. In her youth she attended a French-speaking elementary school and an Arabic speaking high school. She was exceptionally intelligent – after placing fourth highest in the University of Egypt's entrance examinations, she took her degree there in French literature. My father, an orthopedic surgeon, was so secular he was, privately, an atheist. He staked great value on critical thinking and logical analysis. He wanted us to be comfortable with reality and not seek to augment it with fantasy. He believed that what he regarded as superstition, which stemmed from insularity, was a source of many problems in the world. He felt it incumbent to broaden our exposure to "life". Accordingly, when I was about eight, he took my brother and me to a cadaver room at the medical school to show us "Death" – to show us, in other words, that death is not a romantic or mysterious affair, but a scientific one. I had nightmares for years.

Yet, while my father might be said to have worshipped

---

[2]For example, in 1961, Nasser dismissed two Grand Imams at Al-Azhar University and relegated to himself the power to appoint future Grand Imams.

science and logic, he was in every respect a warm and upright man. He raised us with the value of tolerance, teaching us to respect all religious beliefs, including those of Christians and Jews. Our own practice of Islam was negligble – it was limited to a cultural celebration of the Ramadan fast and its corresponding feast. In more traditional Islamic families, boys start learning how to pray at the age of seven, and are strongly encouraged to pray regularly and go to the mosque at the age of ten. I did not regularly visit the mosque until my latter teenage years.

In 1970, Anwar Sadat succeeded Nasser and relaxed his predecessor's travel restrictions. Since my father was well-regarded in the medical community, he seized the opportunity to work abroad regularly, particularly in Algeria, Saudi Arabia, and Libya – often for extensive lengths of time. During those periods I busied myself with poetry, chess and playing with friends, some of whom were Christian. I loved my father, but as a result of his absences, my uncle Kamal – a famous actor and director in Egyptian cinema – became my role model.

Kamal graduated from the Sorbonne as a Theatrical Director. He used to collaborate regularly with my mother – she would translate French dramatic works into Arabic and assisted my uncle to produce them. I enjoyed observing the rehearsals. Often, he would show up at my school to watch me in class. The students and teachers knew him and paid me extra respect. When my uncle and I would walk down the street, passers-by would salute him, ask him for his autograph, and invite us to meals. He was not only charismatic and successful, but generous with time and money. Many families would have him over for the holiday feasts, and when he came he would typically give each child the equivalent of 100 dollars. He liked to listen to me recite poems. He helped me with handwriting and public speaking, working with me on a regular basis to improve them.

Egypt's "Revival of Islam"

In the early 1970s, the words "Revival of Islam" were increasingly heard. This happened for several reasons. During and after the OPEC oil embargo (America's first energy crisis), the price of petroleum skyrocketed, leading to astronomical profits for OPEC nations, especially Saudi Arabia. I remember the price per barrel jumping from $12 to $42. We heard about them getting rich from news reports, and saw Egyptians return from employment there flush with cash. Those who worked in Egypt – medicine, engineering, finance – might earn 200£ per month, but in Saudi Arabia the same position would often net them 10,000£ per month. As a result, the gap between rich and poor increased, strengthening the sense of contrast that Egyptians felt. The infusions of foreign cash had the secondary effect of increasing inflation. Prices rose and basic necessities became more expensive. In response, an increasing percentage of the Egyptian skilled labor force was compelled to work in Saudi Arabia. A cycle developed which created, in essence, an unhealthy dependency on the Saudis for propping-up the Egyptian economy. In return, the Saudis gained additional leverage over Egyptian policies. In the 1940s, the Saudis were struggling economically – Egyptians used to contribute money to the Saudis so that they could maintain the cover for the Kaaba (the holiest building in Islam). Money flowed from Egypt to Saudi Arabia. By the 1970s, the situation had reversed. OPEC nations were a source of marvel throughout the Arab world, not only from the perspective of wealth, but also from pride at Arab resistance to the US. Since the Saudis practiced Salafism and implemented Sharia law throughout the kingdom, many believed that the Saudis were rewarded by Allah with wealth and respect in recognition of their strict devotion.

Sadat himself never pursued Nasser's socialist, anti-American agenda. Subsequent to the 1973 war, he actually sent the Soviet military advisors home. When he ascended to power, Sadat sought immediately to limit the influence of the Nasserists, and did so by releasing their enemies – the Islamists that Nasser had imprisoned. Because the majority of the mosques were strictly controlled by the government, Sadat underestimated the threat the Islamists would pose if they could freely preach in their enclaves. In fact, the release of imprisoned Islamists might have reflected a genuine wish on Sadat's part to ease restrictions on speech and religion.

Sadat began to act on his desire for a rapprochement with the US, and did so by utilizing these government-controlled mosques to disseminate messages of peace with America and Israel. In consequence, the Islamists that Sadat had released earlier began to make noises that he was un-Islamic, even an infidel. They asserted that a good Muslim should never accept a civil-service post, for example, because such a post assisted an un-Islamic regime. Sadat was forced to respond to this attack on his reputation. He would occasionally refer to himself as "Muhammad Sadat", and to show good faith, he further eased the suppression of radical, unregulated mosques.

The erstwhile freed Islamists were hardly satisfied by Sadat's Islamic façade. As might be expected, the radical incitement began to permeate more mainstream establishments. Sadat was still able to inhibit Islamist violence, but he failed to combat their incitement at prayers. Mainstream mosques encountered a similar dilemma to that faced by Sadat. Previously, these establishments focused on the basic "Five Pillars of Islam" and little else – they were not especially interested in doctrinal complexity. Islamists began to preach from their isolated pulpits that the conventional mosques fostered a diluted Islam and that their members were weak Muslims. Day-in and day-out they would carry on about Sharia and the Caliphate. Mainstream institutions, too, were forced to defend their reputation against these allegations by making a public show of their Islamic devotion, and so, the Revival got underway.

It started mildly enough and has never really ceased. It developed in various institutions at various times and at various rates, but it constituted, on the whole, a perceptible collective shift. At first there was an awakened pride in Islam, followed by an insistence on return to ritual (e.g. regular mosque attendance). Earlier, in the 1950s and 60s, it was very rare for an employee to interrupt his work so that he could pray. If he did so, it was perceived as bizarre and treated, at times, with scorn. In the 70s, it became much more common and fellow employees who opted not to pray would express approval of their co-worker's devotion. Soon, television shows would be interrupted with the Islamic call-to-prayer. It lasted five minutes and we hated it because it interrupted exciting soccer games. During these moments, it was common to turn on the radio and listen to the event because radio broadcasts weren't interrupted.

As time passed, Imams began to advocate that women wear the *hijab*, or head scarf. It suffices to simply compare class photographs from Nasser's time to those taken between 1970s and the present. Before, the *hijab* was hardly worn, but after Islamists gained influence, many women in the photographs can be observed wearing them. Similarly, husbands in the 50s usually wore a wedding ring made of gold. Later, silver became the metal of choice, because a certain hadith proclaimed the wearing of gold to be un-Islamic.

> *Gold and silk are allowed for the women of my nation (Muslims) but they are forbidden for men.*
> Ahmed, al-Nassaii, and al-Tirmizi

Hatred of non-Muslims, especially Jews, increased as well; this was true particularly in mosques not under government control. Imams began to preach more regularly that Jews were a race of pigs and monkeys which poisoned Muhammad, that they should be fought until the end of days. Under Nasser, such forms of religious preaching were uncommon. Popular songs in the 50s were not anti-Semitic, whereas a few years ago, in the 21st century, a hit song in

Egypt was entitled "I Hate Israel". This is not to say that Jew-hatred never existed, of course. But in earlier periods it was a relatively muted political issue which coalesced around an Arab identity rather than an Islamic one. The former is much easier to treat than the latter.

Eventually, mainstream mosques, too, began to speak of *Sharia* and even promote it in favor of secular government. Soon, they began to passively justify violence. They may not have "given you the knife" (so to speak), but they played their role in establishing and promulgating a theoretical foundation for brutality.

In the Revival's first phase, however, its effect on society was less one of incitement than it was a re-invigoration of strict Salafi practices and beliefs. It was a sense of pride in Islamic power, and it was at this time, as the "Islamic Revival" got under way, that I entered high school.

Adolescence

I used to sit between two friends: Nagi Anton (a Christian) and Muhammad Amin, (an atheist). Nagi and I used to "gang up" on Amin in debates, seeking to prove to him the existence of God. I enjoyed these theological disputes and began to study religion in an effort to "win" more of them. Soon, Muslim and Christian students began to meet informally for theological sparring. It was, for the most part, friendly. Occasionally a participant would insult an opponent, leading to animosity, but that was relatively rare. Muslim classmates chose me to lead the debates against the Christian students. I was a good debater and basked in the high esteem in which my classmates held me. I studied the Old and New Testaments in order to find ammunition with which I could best my Christian adversaries. The debates actually led to an ironic situation where I knew more of the Bible than I did about Islam itself. Such contests were innocent enough. My only goal was to win them and maintain the respect of my schoolmates.

At the same time (between the ages of 15 and 16), it happened that I started to think about God more spiritually. This happened while studying the structure and function of the DNA molecule as part of a homework assignment for biology class. I couldn't believe that the grace and organization of life's central molecule was some evolutionary coincidence. It must have resulted from the unlimited power of a divine architect. I looked in the Quran for confirmations of my spiritual wonder at nature and found them.

> Behold! in the creation of the heavens and the earth, and the alternation of night and day,- there are indeed Signs for men of understanding…. Men who celebrate the praises of Allah, standing, sitting, and lying down on their sides, and contemplate the (wonders of) creation in the heavens and the earth, (with the thought): "Our Lord! Not for naught Hast Thou created (all) this! Glory to Thee! Give us salvation from the penalty of the Fire."
> {Quran 3:190-191}

My father was often abroad and the influence of his atheism had been receding. It is strange, looking back, that while I shared my father's attraction to science, it led me in the opposite, religious direction.

My exposure to religion during the debates, the esteem of my peers, and my wonder at nature combined to fuel an earnest interest in Islam. The community as a whole seemed to give me more respect as I sought to be a more dedicated Muslim. I still did not go to the mosque very often, but I would pray at home. If we were watching a soccer game or eating supper, I would stop and pray in everyone's presence. I would go to wash my hands, feet, face and head, and then return to place the *sijadda*, or prayer mat, on the ground, adjusting it to face Mecca. As I was praying I would receive complements from others in the room. Some of my friends went further. They walked to mosque prayers – the farther away the mosque, the better. It was believed to be a sign of devotion to walk to a distant mosque. Often, they would count their footsteps and relate the total as proof of their faith.

Time passed, and I recall the first time I looked at a Christian with disdain. We were in Arabic language class reading a passage from an obligatory textbook called *Al-Shaichan* ("The Two Wise Old Men").[3]The book referenced what the hadiths suppose were Prophet Muhammad's words:

> *I have been instructed by Allah to declare war and fight all mankind until they say No God except Allah and Muhammad is the prophet of Allah.*
> Sahih Al-Buchary and Muslim

This passage can be found in *Sahih Al-Buchary* and *Sahih Muslim* – two of the most important Sunni Hadith collections. Christian students went to their own Religion class and Muslim students went to theirs. But this class wasn't Religion – it was Arabic – so Nagi was present. The implications of the Prophet's supposed words dawned on me. I turned to him and said: "If we applied Islam correctly we should be doing this to you".

The summer after high school, I attended prayers regularly at a local mosque.

Medical School

I entered the medical school at Cairo University when I was 17 (Egypt didn't have the same concept of "undergraduate" typical of the West). Naturally, I continued to pursue my recently acquired fervor for Islam. At the time, an Islamic

---

[3]The textbook was written by Taha Hussein who was the Dean of the School of Arabic Language at Cairo University. A very well known scholar, Taha was blind since childhood, learning the Quran by verbal repetition at Al-Azhar school. Al-Azhar, better known as a university, actually consists of two parts – the university and a religious school for children. Taha didn't like the teaching at Al-Azhar and left because it was too fundamentalist. He was so critical of Al-Azhar that some called him an apostate. The hadith cited here refers to the first two Caliphs, Abu Bakr and Umar.

organization called *Jamaa Islamiya*[4] had been gaining a
foothold at the school. Although it was later classified as a
terrorist group, *Jamaa*'s activities were perfectly legal then.
They began by receiving permission to build a small prayer
room inside the medical school, which quickly developed
into a small mosque. Shortly thereafter, a library was
added to the "mosque" where *Jamaa* members promoted
Salafist books.

Clearly, Egypt's "Revival of Islam" had made its way to the
medical school. *Jamaa* members would not only preach in
their "mosque". As its influence spread, the group started a
tradition of meeting in the morning lecture hall 45 minutes
before the teacher arrived, where they would lecture on
Islamic topics from the podium. Most Muslim students
thought it a good thing, but more secular ones found it
annoying, and Christian students were wholly intimidated
into silence. It was the custom at the medical school to refer
to professors by their title and first name. One day, "Dr.
Edward", a Christian, was unable to begin his lecture because
the *Jamaa* speaker had not finished. When Dr. Edward
stepped up to the podium and asked *Jamaa* to conclude, six
members called the professor an infidel and started to berate
him. Dr. Edward was pushed off the podium, fell, and broke
his arm. Secular students were disgusted and Christian
students were terrified. The reaction of Muslim students was
mixed. Some approved of it, others thought it was excessive.
Personally, I regretted the violence; but because I was a
Muslim, I felt that *Jamaa* had the right to preach in class and
that the professor should not have "provoked" them. I was
not yet a member.

Behind one of the two main lecture halls at the medical school
was a cadaver room – the exact one that my father showed
me as a child. Sometimes *Jamaa* lecturers would point in the
direction of the cadaver room from the podium, as evidence

---

[4]Also transliterated as *al-Gama'a al-Islamiyya, Gamaat Islamiya, Jamaat al Islamiya,
al-Jam_'ah al-Isl_miyah,* etc. The name should not be confused with similarly-named
Islamist group based in Indonesia.

of the earthly world's expendable imperfection. For the non-believers and unobservant Muslims, they would utilize the same example to hector us about Hell. The passages they read would echo in the halls and in our minds:

> *For those who do not follow Allah, garments of fire shall be cut out for them (in the life to come); burning water will be poured over their heads causing all that is within their bodies, as well as the skins, to melt away. And they shall be held by iron grips; and every time they try in their anguish to come out of it, they shall be returned there to and (be told): "Taste suffering through fire (to the full)!"*
> {Quran 22:19-22}

The dead bodies in the cadaver room were used to show us that only the second life is important – earthly life is meaningless. Martyrdom guaranteed entrance to Paradise:

> *Those who desire the life of the present and its glitter, to them we shall pay [the price of] their deeds therein, without diminution, . . . (yet) it is they who, in the life to come, shall have nothing but the fire—for in vain shall be all good things that they have done in this [world], and worthless all that they ever did.*
> {Quran 11:15-16}

By a strange irony, *Jamaa* employed exactly the same example as my father had years earlier, in order to teach me precisely the opposite lesson.

As its influence grew, *Jamaa Islamiya* began to intervene with the secular traditions of the medical school. They insisted on separate seating in the lecture halls for men and women, and sometimes forcibly separated students who did not comply. Occasionally, they would use violence to stop students from playing music or singing, activities the members considered "un-Islamic".

One naturally asks, "Why medical students?" Westerners are often astonished to observe highly accomplished Muslim doctors in the terrorist ranks. These include Dr. Ayman Al-Zawahiri (surgeon) second in command of Al-Qaeda, Dr. Abdul-Aziz Al-Rantisi of HAMAS (pediatrician, now deceased), and most recently, a group of doctors (including a neurosurgeon) who planned recent attacks on Scottish and English transportation systems.[5] Doctors almost universally agree to the Hippocratic Oath and swear by another of Hippocrates' maxims: "First, do no harm." How then could a group like *Jamaa Islamiya* gain traction in a medical school?

It is actually not a surprise to me that I became radicalized there. Our medical schools at that time were a vanguard of fundamentalism in most Egyptian universities.

Medical students are often more attracted to religion because they see the power of God in nature on a regular basis. They study the miraculous structure and function of the human body, after all. Certainly, for me and many others this wonder was a significant motivating element.

Once attracted to religion, Islamists inside the school fostered in students an abnormal fear of mortality; because we witnessed death so closely in patients and regularly worked with cadavers, they were able to play on our proximity to it. We were encouraged to think about the next world. Islamists seized the opportunity to continuously remind us of the torture that would await us in the grave (*Azab Al-Kabr*) or in the afterlife (*Jahanam*) if we did not obey their religious teachings. Some students were influenced by this approach, others less so.

Because we worked with sick patients, Islamists would also claim that we would be punished in the present for our lack of devotion by acquiring the diseases of the patients. Allah would curse us not only in the afterlife, but in this life. This tactic sometimes worked with students who feared disease more than usual.

Finally, Islamists would manipulate our sense of guilt. Many students felt particularly relieved that they were spared the

[5]Russel Goldman, "Can Terrorists Trained as Doctors Slip into the United States?", *ABC News Online*, July 4, 2007, http://abcnews.go.com/US/story?id=3343370&page=1

often-horrible illnesses of the patients they treated and would naturally thank Allah for it. Islamists insisted that strict devotion to their Islamic agenda was the only acceptable expression of gratitude; anything else was insulting to Allah.

It is not surprising that Islamists would target medical schools in the first place. Students are bright and idealistic, yet hard-working and practical. They are naturally concerned with issues of life, death, pain, and salvation.

A New Recruit

Eventually in my first year I was approached by a promising member of *Jamaa* named Muchtar. He was in his fourth year and known in the group as *amir*, or "prince". The title was short for "Prince of the Believers"[6] , a term taken from early writings about the Islamic caliphate. Determination to serve Allah overcame my hesitancy that remained from witnessing the incident with Dr. Edward, and I agreed to join them in what I thought would be a commonplace gathering for prayer. En route to the mosque, Muchtar impressed upon me a concept that he called *al-fikr kufr* – that one becomes an infidel (*kufr*) by thinking critically (*fikr*). One's brain is similar to a donkey, he elaborated – you can ride it to the palace of Allah, but you must leave it outside when you enter.

It presently became clear why Muchtar had prepared me. Before the service all the new candidates were instructed to line-up shoulder-to-shoulder and foot-to-foot. Muhammad Omar, the cleric, scrutinized us for fifteen minutes to make sure there were no gaps, and then proclaimed, *"Truly Allah loves those who fight for His Cause in battle array, as if they were a solid cemented structure"* {Quran 61:4}. After prayers I was advised to visit the library regularly and begin reading Salafi texts, which I did.

---

[6]It is short for *Amir Al-Moomenin*, a term employed during the Islamic Caliphate.

Certainly, *Jamaa Islamiya* counted women as members. The women prayed in a separate room and were very dedicated. They wore the *hijab* and the men related to them as comrades or "sisters in arms". There was no dating between members under any circumstances. Before I met her, my wife was actually invited to join them. She declined; perhaps her father's Sufi faith granted her a stronger immunity to the group than the atheist inclinations of my own father. Yet, if Islamists advocated stoning women for adultery and limiting their rights, what could possibly attract women to the group? Obviously, they suffered from denial, but there were incentives that created that denial, that overcame a basic aversion to the world their "brothers" envisioned.

As a new member, I was sometimes asked to speak with women students who might be prospective candidates for *Jamaa*. Sex in paradise was less of an enticement for them, but fear of Hell played a significant role. They would sometimes cry when I laid out the hellfire that awaited weak Muslims. Many women were terrified of it, no less than the men. Also like the men, women got respect for being members. Those from poorer backgrounds sometimes felt insecure in relation to affluent girls and sought to claim a measure of superiority over them. Islamism gave them that power. They might not have the wealth, but they had religious devotion and found favor in the eyes of Allah. Poorer girls allowed themselves to believe that their well-to-do counterparts were spoiled, pampered and weak. Societal norms also played a role. Young men wanted to date secular girls, but when it came to marriage, men often sought religious ones. Observant women were more likely to be chaste – an important concern in Arab culture. Mothers would actually encourage girls to wear the *hijab* because it encouraged men to seek them out as marriage partners and not for friendship and dating.

As for myself, after several months of attending *Jamaa*'s sermons and reading their Salafi books, I began to change dramatically. I grew a beard, lost all sense of humor, became aloof and judgmental. My father and mother tried to convince me to relax my religious views and to leave *Jamaa*. Because Salafi Islam forbids many forms of art and music, my relationship with my uncle Kamal also suffered. I couldn't forgive him for his devotion to the un-Islamic diversions of theatre and film.

Phases of Indoctrination

An innocent person cannot be changed into to a violent jihadist in one day. An individual changes incrementally and subtly – it is a gradual mental process which occurs, broadly, in three stages: Hatred, Suppression of Conscience, and Desensitization (or acceptance) of Violence.

Hatred

It would be difficult to kill an innocent person if one didn't hate that person first. Hatred toward the "Infidels" is not only promoted by jihadist groups like *Jamaa*, but also in mainstream Islamic teaching. The books, the jurisprudence, and the commentaries assist in creating this hatred. Here are only few examples:

> *O ye who believe! Take not the Jews and the Christians for your friends and protectors: They are but friends and protectors to each other. And he amongst you that turns to them (for friendship) is of them. Verily Allah guideth not a people unjust.*
> {Quran 5:51}

> *Say: "Shall I point out to you something much worse than this, (as judged) by the treatment it received from Allah, those who incurred the curse of Allah and His wrath (the Jews), those of whom some He transformed into apes and swine, those who worshipped evil - these are (many times) worse in rank, and far more astray from the even path!"*
> {Quran 5:60}

Those who say that God is Christ the son of Mary are Infidels.
{Quran 5:17}

This following hadith has special significance for me. When I later lived in Saudi Arabia, I remember the Wahabbis had selected it for publication in one of their small booklets. They would freely distribute these in order to teach Muslims about Islam.

Prophet Muhammad has said: "Do not initiate the Salam (peace greeting) to the Jews and Christians and whenever you meet any of them in a road, force them to its narrowest alley."
Sahih Muslim

This teaching is also promoted in the mainstream Islamic books that are used by young Muslims in the US.[7]

Suppression of Conscience

Similarly, if instructed to kill someone, a person might feel that such an act is unethical, even if he did hate the potential victim. It would be difficult to perform the murder in this case if the would-be murderer couldn't overcome his conscience.

Islamism suppresses the conscience of its adherents by pressuring them to accept, promote, and praise acts that are entirely at odds with a normal sense of decency and justice, simply because they are recorded in the religious books. We used to praise Prophet Muhammad for marrying a girl of seven when he was 52 years old (as written in Al-Buchary). Similarly, we openly advocated stoning women to death, killing apostates (converts from Islam), enslaving female war prisoners and having sex with them as concubines (*Ma Malakat Aymanicum*). All of these practices are an integral part of mainstream Islamic teaching – if we advocated them,

---

[7]See *Tafseer Ibn Kathir* and *Minhaj al-Muslim* by *Abu Bakr Jabir Al-Jaza'iry*.

Paradise awaited us; if we even questioned these beliefs, then we faced eternal damnation in Hell.

Desensitization to Violence

In the final stage, a person might hesitate to follow-through on the murder if he weren't sufficiently desensitized to violence. Thus, the third phase in the creation of a jihadist is the removal of any aversion to it.

Again, Salafi religious interpretations lead the way. Current, mainstream Islamic teaching insists that good Muslims must declare war on "infidels". Non-believers are to be offered three options: to convert to Islam, to pay the *jizya* (a humiliating poll tax), or be slain. Mainstream and so-called moderate Islamic books, such as the *Fiqh Al-Sunna*, insist that a Muslim who fails to pray five times per day must repent or be tortured and killed (See Fiqh Al-Sunna by Saiid Sabeq, Part I Prayer Section). Ironically, at the beginning of the third part of the same book, the author maintained that Islam is all about peace. Islamists, Islamic scholars, and many Muslims consider these texts *as applicable today as they were in the past.*

Consider a few examples:

> *After the raid on a Jewish tribe … the disciples of Muhammad brought Kinanah Ibn Alrabbia in front of Muhammad as he knew the place of the treasures of the Jewish tribe (Bani Al-Nuder). The man denied that he knew the place of such treasures ... The prophet (pbuh) said to one of his disciples (Alzubeer Ibn Alawam) "torture him until you root out and extract all that he has" ... So Zubayr kindled a fire on Kinanah's chest, twirling it with his firestick until Kinanah was near death, then prophet Muhammad pushed him forcibly toward Muhammad Ibn Maslama to kill him ... The latter beheaded him (to satisfy the prophet).*
> Alsira Alnabawia ('The Life of the Prophet") by Ibn Hisham

There was a woman named Fatima Bint Rabiaa who was well-known as Um Kerfa. All her children were great leaders among the Arab tribes. She was one of the most respected women in the Arab society and was an example for dignity so that when two tribes had a fight they immediately stopped fighting if she intervened to make peace by sending her head cover on a post in between the fighting groups. This woman was a poet and she used to recite poems against Muhammad. In the 6th year after Muhammad left Mecca to Medina she sent one of the best disciples, Zaid Ibn Harisa in a raid to punish her. Zyad tied her legs with rope and then tied her between two camels until they split her in two. And then after beheading the dead body he carried the dead body to Medina and put her head on a post to satisfy the Prophet.

Al-Tabakat Al-Kubra by Ibn Saad Bab
"The Raid of Zaid Ibn Harisa to Um Kerfa"

Critics will contend that the Old and New Testaments also contain violent passages. But Judaism and Christianity teach these verses in historical context, as no longer practicable, to be understood metaphorically or in the worldview of an earlier period of civilization. Islam today fails to furnish a counter-balanced understanding. Violent exhortations are still acceptable and applicable in countries or communities that implement Sharia law. They are not only found in the texts; Islamic scholars agree almost *unanimously* about the validity and violent interpretation of such injunctions.

Once a Muslim accepts cruelty at the psychological level, it is a natural step to see it as a tool for a larger ideological program. In the medical school, some of us stopped at the level of hatred, others suppressed their conscience but went no further, while others reached the last stage, ready to wage jihad. All of these *phases* are necessary to manufacture the cruel mentalities that we see today, prepared to target large numbers of innocent people. But if these are phases that a normal person experiences on the path to terror, it remains to identify the *tactics* used by Islamist groups to bring about such a transformation.

Tactics of Indoctrination

It is very difficult to convey to non-Muslims the attraction to radical Islam that believers can feel. It is a multi-faceted experience, greater than the sum of its parts. Individuals can be drawn to militant Islam for different reasons – no single element of Islamism by itself can explain why young Muslims around the world fall victim to it daily. The only requirement is a willingness to serve Allah and Islam. I remember a feeling of exhilaration at *Jamaa*'s unity and vision, the singularity of purpose and the fearlessness the group displayed in the face of opposition from government and moderates. It was a feeling of raw power – the power to change the course of history and to sweep current society aside. It was, as some might say, not unlike a drug, an addiction, but it was more: their program of religious study and their sermons spoke to my awakening interest in the Divine.

For Jews and Christians, the Bible is a testament to God's covenant, to his deeds, to what he said to other people. God speaks to Moses, Moses paraphrases to his people, and the Old Testament tells us what Moses said. It is a history, a chronicle. Both the Old Testament and the New have been translated into countless languages and each translation is acceptable for prayer and study because the words themselves are less important than their meaning – it is the content that matters. For example, one of Judaism's greatest scholars – Philo of Alexandria – based his writings chiefly on the Pentateuch (the Greek translation of the Old Testament); it is still a matter of debate whether he knew Hebrew. Similarly, Christians in America read the New Testament in English. They do not feel compelled to read it in Greek unless they are theologians and do not feel themselves to be "less Christian" as a result.

The Quran is different. It is the actual word of God, directly transmitted to each believer individually. It is as if each believer is Moses being personally addressed by the Lord.

And because God spoke these words in Arabic, translations of the Quran are regarded as mere facsimiles.

This power of the Quran is augmented by the role that poetry plays in Arab culture. In the West, a quick examination of the sales ranking of books shows that poetry is not especially popular. Of course there are devoted readers, but their number is small. In the Arab world poetry competitions are mainstream. Poems are read avidly; people still weep when they hear them, and children memorize collections as part of their education. Traditionally, Bedouin culture in Arabia didn't produce a musical tradition that spawned complex and endless variations of mathematized harmony. In the visual arts, a representation of Allah or the Prophet was and still is regarded as idolatrous. Human portraits only began to be permitted under the Ottomans. It was in literature, epic and lyrical poetry, that Arabic culture excelled. The language lent itself to a long and influential tradition.

Yet it is not merely the voice and language of the Quran that are utilized by Islamists. They deftly exploit a number of themes to bring young Muslims into their organizations.

Suppression of Critical Thinking

The first tactic that *Jamaa Islamiya* employed was to pressure me to suppress critical thought. I have already mentioned how Muchtar encouraged me to "leave my brain at the door", and his use of the phrase, *al fikr kufr*[8]("thinking critically makes one an infidel"). Actually, the Quran encourages critical thinking in numerous verses. However, the leaders of Jamaa focused on a specific verse:

> *He cannot be questioned for His acts, but they will be questioned (for theirs).*
> {Quran: 21:23}

---

[8]A saying made more effective by its use of the same three letters in its Arabic root.

In other words, nobody can question Allah about his instructions, decisions, or actions. The suppression of my critical thinking was *the most important factor* that trapped me in the path of Jihadism. All other techniques of indoctrination are dependent upon it. Jihadists understand that it takes time for new recruits to lose their capacity to think critically, so leaders prefer to keep members in the group where they can gradually erode it. Ultimately, however, one cannot become a jihadist if reason and objectivity aren't thoroughly crushed.

Superiority

Another factor that played a major role in our Islamization was to convince us that adherence to Islam and Sharia is the best way to regain the "superiority of Islam". They argued that the early Islamic conquests succeeded in less than a century not only because Muslims practiced jihad against external enemies, but because they applied strict Islamic law at home. If we modern Muslims did the same, we thought we could subjugate the rest of the world again. Our inferior international status and our economic problems would be a thing of the past. Islamists in *Jamaa* supported these arguments with many citations from the Quran, the Hadiths, and other Islamic resources.

Islamists consider other Muslims who do not engage in jihad to be inferior. Recall how leaders of *Jamaa* such as Muchtar were commonly addressed as *amir*, or "prince", a term which refers to the leaders of the early Islamic Caliphate. The use of this expression encouraged members to avoid integrating into wider society, because it was composed of "lesser" Muslims; they did not practice Islam as strictly as we did.

State of War

It was not left up to recruits to decide if there was a war with the infidels. Jihadist leaders insisted we were already at war with non-Muslims. Adherents and potential-adherents were faced with the option of bravely joining the battle, or cowardly avoiding it. We have seen how the Imam at the mosque meticulously instructed us to stand "shoulder-to-shoulder and foot-to-foot". At that time we felt like soldiers, tasked with fighting for Allah against the enemies of Islam. Our minds would envision the victories of the early Islamic conquests. During the prayer, I used to picture myself as a knight of Allah, standing with fellow warriors as "one cemented structure".

Sex and Paradise

In order to brainwash new recruits, Islamists exploit sex in two ways: young men are deprived of it and at the same time enticed with it. It may be termed Sex Deprivation Syndrome (SDS). Broadly speaking, students find it very difficult to marry because of financial limitations. Marriage carries with it great expenses in the Middle East. It is not culturally acceptable for a young man to marry before he graduates and secures employment. Further, the Quran was utilized to prohibit pre-marital sex:

> ...and who never invoke any (imaginary) deity side by side with God, and do not take any human beings life – (the life) which God has willed to be sacred - otherwise than in (the pursuit of) justice, and do not commit adultery. And (know that) he who commits aught thereof shall (not only) meet with a full requital (but) shall have his suffering doubled on Resurrection Day: for on that (Day) he shall abide in ignominy.
> {Quran 25:68-69}

Similarly, release of sexual desire in any other physiological manner is also forbidden by most Islamic scholars. In combination, these factors create a great deal of sexual suppression and frustration among young Muslim men. By themselves, sexual restrictions were not enough to sway us toward jihad, so jihadists directed our attention to the pornographic accounts in Salafi Islamic writings. Sexual release might be nearly impossible in this life, but it was readily available in Paradise. Consider:

Narrated Anas: "The Prophet used to go round (have sexual relations with) all his wives in one night, and he had nine wives."
　Sahih al-Buchary

Narrated Anas: "that Prophet Muhammad used to have sex with all of his 11 wives in only one hour of a day or a night … and he said that Muhammad has been given the power of 30 men in having sex."
　Sahih al-Buchary

In paradise: When the Muslim enters the room to have sex with the first lady of the 72 Hur (beautiful ladies with wide eyes and white skin), he will find her waiting on the bed … He will not become bored at having sex with her and she will not become bored of having sex with him … and every time he has sex with her he will find her a virgin again … and his penis will never relax (i.e. will be continuously erect) after the coitus … Some disciples asked the prophet, "Are we going to have sex in the paradise …?" Muhammad said "Yes, and I swear with the name of the one who controls my soul and body (Allah) that every time the man will finish his turn at sex with her … she will return back a virgin."
　Tafseer Ibn Kathir

A man was sleeping in the house of Aisha (the youngest wife of the prophet) and he ejaculated while sleeping. The concubine of Aisha saw him while he was cleaning it (the semen) with water … She spoke to Aisha who explained to the man that she used to scrub the semen of the Prophet directly with her nails after it dries up.
　Sahih Muslim, Book of Tahara

The ladies of the paradise awaiting the followers of Muhammad are so beautiful to the degree that light shines from their faces, their bodies are as soft as silk, they are white in colour and they wear green clothes and golden jewelry… These beautiful ladies say to the believers when they enter the paradise … "we are eternal for you (to enjoy us) …We are very soft and will never get unhappy. We are continuously ready (for sex) and we are always satisfied and will never be discontent … So blessed is this man who will have us and we will have him."
　Tafseer Ibn Kathir

These texts were in the *Jamaa* library. We were encouraged to read them and believe them literally. Islamists constantly decry the West's export of lewdness and easy sex. Western scholars often concur and chastise their societies for it. However, Islamists use the sexual lewdness in Islamic writings in place of the lewdness they fight against in the West. In combination, sexual prohibitions and enticements help drive some young Muslim men into a fever for jihad (which guarantees them sex in Paradise).

The striking difference in the percentage of suicide bombers between Shia and Sunni Muslims further elucidates this problem. In the last few years, it has become obvious that young Sunni Muslims have contributed to suicide bombings significantly more than their Shia Muslims. We can attribute this phenomenon, in part at least, to the fact that young Shia Muslims are permitted *Zawaj Mutta*, a brief 'temporary marriage' for pre-marital sexual relations.[9] Young Sunni Muslims do not have this option, since the Sunni branch does not recognize *Mutta* at all. In other words, young Shia Muslims do not need to martyr themselves in suicide attacks in order to have sex in Paradise. Unlike many young Sunni Muslims, young Shias can easily have sex on earth. However, it should be noted that Shia Muslims can still conduct suicide bombings if their *Margeia*, or highest religious authorities, order them to do so.

Sex Deprivation Syndrome is not the only factor that causes Jihadism, but it is a significant contributing factor for many young Sunni Muslims. I experienced it personally; leaders of Islamic terrorist organizations regularly promise to their martyrs that they will enjoy the *Hur* or "white ladies" in the afterlife.

---

[9]This does not mean that the author endorses *Zawaj Mutta*.

Prophet Muhammad as Role Model

Being a dedicated Muslim, I dreamt of emulating the Prophet Muhammad in word and deed. Young Muslim men everywhere typically feel the same way and are encouraged to do so, based on the following Quranic verse:

> *"Ye have indeed in the Messenger of Allah a beautiful pattern (of conduct) for any one whose hope is in Allah and the Final Day, and who engages much in the Praise of Allah. "*
> {Quran 33:21}

The Quran has many positive examples of Muhammad's conduct; we will return to his role more thoroughly in the final chapter on reformation. However, *Jamaa Islamiya* (and Islamists in general) exploited purported instances of Muhammad's abusive conduct to encourage us in jihad. It is essential to keep in mind that very few of these examples employed by jihadists are found in the Quran – they come from hadiths and much later writings.

Here are some of passages that *Jamaa* utilized:

> *Allah granted Rayhanah of the (Jewish) Qurayza to His Messenger as booty, but only after she had been forced to watch him decapitate her father and brother, had seen her mother hauled off to be raped, and her sisters sold into slavery.*
> Al-Tabari

> *After Muhammad attacked the Jews of Bani Khriza he killed all their men and divided the women for sexual pleasure among Muslims and enslaved their children and took their money and treasure.*
> Sahih al-Buchary (Kitab al-Maghazy)

> *One day a woman came to Prophet Muhammad (pbuh) and said to him "Do you have a desire in my body (for sex)? If so … I am offering myself to you … Muhammad's daughter said, "This lady does not have any dignity so she offers herself to a man!"…The Prophet said to his daughter "This lady is better than you … as she wanted to be with the Prophet of Allah so she offered herself to him".*
> Sunan Ibn Maga (Kitab al-Nikah)

These verses are widely propagated by Salafists; we were encouraged to read them in *Jamaa*'s library at the medical school. They assist Islamists with the indoctrination tactics of superiority, state of war, and sexual deprivation.

Fear of Hell

The leaders of *Jamaa* and other Islamic scholars managed to manipulate our minds effectively by using the graphic descriptions of Hell in religious writings. Torture in the Quran is not an abstract concept. The descriptions are vivid and gruesomely poetic.

> *But those of the left hand (did not obey Allah and Muhammad or follow them)—how unhappy those of the left hand. They will be in the scorching hot wind and boiling water, under the shadow of thick black smoke, neither cool nor agreeable. …They will be gathered together on a certain day which is predetermined. Then you, the erring and the deniers will eat Zaqum (a thorny tree), fill your bellies with it, and drink scalding water, lapping it up like female camels raging of thirst and disease. Such will be their entertainment, their welcome on the Day of Doom … the welcome of boiling water and the entertainment of roasting in Hell. This is the ultimate truth.*
> {Quran 56:41-57}

> *For we have truly made it as a trial to torment the disbelievers. Zaqum is a horrible thorn tree that grows in Hell. The shoots of its fruit-stalks are like the heads of devils. Truly they (the non-Muslims) will eat it and fill their bellies with it. On top of that they will be given a mixture made of boiling water to drink especially prepared. Then they shall be returned to the Blazing Fire.*
> {Quran 37:63-68}

> *Soon will I fling them into the burning hellfire! And what will explain what hellfire is? It permits nothing to endure, and nothing does it spare! It darkens and changes the color of man, burning the skin! It shrivels and scorches men.*
> {Quran 74:26-29}

We have prepared the doom of Hell and the penalty of torment in the most intense Blazing Fire. For those who reject their Lord is the punishment of Hell: Evil, it is such a wretched destination. When they are flung therein, they will hear the terrible drawing in of their breath and loud moaning even as the flame blazes forth, roaring with rage as it boils up, bursting with fury. Every time a fresh crowd is cast in, Hell's wardens will ask, 'Did no warning come to you?'
    {Quran 67:6-8}

'This,' it will be said, 'is the Fire, which you used to deny!' Is this magic fake? Burn therein, endure the heat; taste it. It's the same whether you bear it patiently or not. This is my retaliation for what you did.
    {Quran 52:14-16}

Those who shall dwell forever in the Fire are given to drink boiling water that tears their bowels to pieces, and cutting their intestines to shreds.
    {Quran 47:15}

With repeated exposure, the consequences of disobeying religious teaching became terrifying. To be saved from such a fate and instead go to Paradise was incentive to perform any deed in the name of Allah.

Restriction of Emotional Outlets

A key tactic of indoctrination was to suppress our ability to appreciate beauty. Islamists prohibited most forms of music, prevented female singing and dancing, and forbade drawing anything with a soul. This suppression had a rigorous theological base in Salafi teaching. Women were also not allowed to wear perfume or make up. We could not disobey because, again, we would spend eternity in Hell.

What is the life of this world but play and amusement? But best is the home in the hereafter, for those who are righteous. Will ye not then understand?
    {Quran 6:32}

"Amusements" – such as music and dancing – were considered evil activities. But once our ability to appreciate beauty was suppressed, we became more vulnerable to accepting ugly and even barbaric teachings.

In short, these tactics are exploited to great effect in order to produce the phases of transformation into a jihadist. When believers hear the Quran in Arabic, they experience these tactical components as the literal word of God expressed in poetry. It can have a stirring effect when read or spoken alone, but in the hands of a gifted cleric, Quranic verses can be mesmerizing.

Doctor "Ayman"

It happened one afternoon that a guest Imam came to deliver a sermon. His topic didn't concern itself with dry details of prayer and fasting. He was fiery and charismatic; his passion was holy war. It was to be fought on all fronts, against all non-believers, without compromise, until all people either converted, submitted to Sharia, or were slain. He made us feel that Islamic victory was possible, that we could make the glorious days of the Islamic conquest return. After the sermon, a fellow member, Tariq Abdul-Muhsin, asked me if I knew the Imam. When I answered that I didn't, he told me that the speaker was Dr. Ayman Al-Zawahiri. Because I was a new member, Tariq offered to introduce me to him.

In person, Al-Zawahiri was very polite and decent with the members of *Jamaa*. It was hard to reconcile his fiery sermons with the quiet man before me, but Zawahiri was only applying a Salafi understanding of a holy verse:

> *Muhammad is the apostle of Allah, and those who are with him are strong against Unbelievers, (but) compassionate amongst each other.*
> {Quran 48:29}

I remember feeling very proud when Zawahiri told me: "Young Muslims like you are the hope for the future return of *Khilafa* [Caliphate or Islamic global dominance]". He made me want to fight for him, to show him my courage and loyalty. Zawahiri himself came from a wealthy, well-known and well-educated family and was a top post-graduate student at the medical school. He was active in a number of Islamist groups so he did not devote all of his time to *Jamaa*. We used to call him "Dr. Ayman".

Dr. Al-Zawahiri's speeches employed Hadiths and Quranic verses to great effect. He was a master at attracting new recruits and inciting them to jihad. It is worthwhile studying his use of Islamic texts in terms of the phases and tactics we have mentioned, particularly hatred, superiority, and war:

> *Fight those who believe neither in Allah nor the Last Day, nor hold that forbidden which hath been forbidden by Allah and His Messenger (Muhammad), nor acknowledge the religion of Truth (Islam), (even if they are) of the People of the Book (Christians and Jews), until they pay the Jizia (Humiliating Poll Tax) with submission, and feel themselves subdued.*
> {Quran 9: 29}

> *But when the forbidden months (a certain four months in the Arabic calendar) are past, then fight and slay the Infidels wherever you find them, and seize them, beleaguer them, and lie in wait for them in every stratagem (to do harm to them); but if they repent (convert from their beliefs to Islam), and establish the regular (Islamic) prayers and practice the regular Zakat (Islamic charity), then open the way for them: for Allah is Oft-forgiving, Most Merciful.*
> {Quran 9:5}

> *Allah hath purchased of the believers their persons and their goods; for theirs (in return) is the garden (of Paradise): they fight in His cause, and slay and are slain: a promise binding on Him in truth, through the Law, the Gospel, and the Qur'an: and who is more faithful to his covenant than Allah. then rejoice in the bargain which ye have concluded: that is the achievement supreme*
> {Quran 9:111}

…when ye meet the Unbelievers, smite at their necks;
   {Quran 47:4}

"So fight them (the Non-Muslims) until there is no more Fitnah (disbelief) and all submit to the religion of Allah alone"
   {Quran 8:39}

"It is He Who hath sent His Messenger (Muhammad) with guidance and the Religion of Truth, to proclaim it and make it superior over all other religions……"
   {Quran 9:33}

Yet, if Zawahiri was a potent speaker, how did he propose to create the world he wanted, and what kind of world did he want to create?

To answer this, we need to say a few words about the differences between Islamist organizations, particularly those in Egypt. The proliferation of such groups is a frequent source of mystification to Westerners, but for all intents and purposes the strategic goal of each organization is the same; they differ primarily in tactical focus. One can find at any moment dozens of such groups in a given nation or geopolitical region. Most collaborate on occasion and are typically on good terms with each other. In Egypt at the time, several such groups were particularly noteworthy, although many others existed.

Islamic Jihad[10], for example, was extremely violent. They would concentrate on the assassination of important political leaders. Their violence was not diffuse, but highly targeted. Also brutal, and broadly so, was *Takfir Wa Al-Hijra*. *"Takfir"* means "consider others as Infidels" while *Al-Hijra* refers to the group's segregation from society. They practiced murder and mass-murder as a matter of policy. When that wasn't possible they engaged in theft, physical assault and intimidation wherever and whenever they could. The group distinguished little between Christians, Jews, and secular Muslims – all three were infidels and impediments to Islamic

---

[10]For our purposes, this group should not be confused with the Palestinian terrorist group of the same name.

world domination. They provided recruits with weapons and didn't particularly care if targets were important on the national level.

On the opposite side of the Islamist spectrum was *Jamaa al-Tabligh Waal-Daawa* (literally, "Party of Messengers"). This group sought societal change toward Islamist rule through grassroots outreach. They did not clearly condemn violence nor deny the violent aspects of Salafi teaching. Members of the organization would travel door-to-door to preach a return to strict Islamic orthodoxy while avoiding political discussion or activity. Another group from a similar mold was *Ansar al-Sunna*, which translates (awkwardly) to "Supporters of Following in Muhammad's Footsteps". Their goal was to emulate Prophet Muhammad in every aspect of life, including those abusive and sexual inclinations described by Salafi writings. They forbade a husband to see his wife completely naked, for example, but encouraged polygamy. They dressed like the Prophet by wearing white clothes, a beard and a short mustache. Members also would apply a cologne called *misk* and utilized a special toothpick (*siwak*) made of sandalwood (to promote healthy gums), because Prophet Muhammad was reputed to have used them.
 The group was obsessed with manners – e.g. eat with the right hand, sit on the floor, finish a glass in three gulps. One can observe this influence in Osama bin Laden's behavior.

Somewhere in the "middle" was the *Muslim Brotherhood*. Their flag illustrates their philosophy. It depicts two swords and beneath them, the Arabic word *Wa-Aiidu* ("prepare"), based on the following verse:

> *Prepare for them (the Infidels) whatever military power you have, so that you insert fear in the hearts of the enemies of Allah.*
> {Quran 8:60}

Although the group assassinated a prime minister and attempted to assassinate Nasser, the organization did not by-and-large participate in violence directly. Bloodshed was not its main tool. They sought to infiltrate politics on the grassroots level and then use democracy to end democracy. Of course, the group was illegal and no candidate for political office could openly run as a brother, but voters usually knew and it was understood within communities which candidate was involved. The Muslim Brotherhood was, and still is, extremely influential.

There remains, at last, *Jamaa Islamiya* (literally, "Islamic Group"). It concentrated on recruiting from society's "best and brightest" by entrenching itself in universities and medical schools. Having done so, *Jamaa* prepared the theoretical foundations for jihad and propagated them to promising students who could best absorb them. Like the Muslim Brotherhood, *Jamaa* didn't participate directly in terror – it would have been counterproductive to provoke a crackdown from school administrations. *Jamaa* was more of a "gateway" group, which, having indoctrinated recruits and equipped them with jihadist knowledge, encouraged them to assume leadership positions in *Islamic Jihad*, the *Muslim Brotherhood*, or to practice jihad in other countries.

Intellectually, Al-Zawahiri was much affected by the teaching of a Muslim Brotherhood leader named Sayyid Qutb. He used to praise Sayyid by saying "Rahimahu Allah" whenever he mentioned his name. The expression means, "May Allah show him mercy and kindness". Qutb was an extremely persuasive writer; he was capable of drawing a picture with his words that left the reader totally captivated. His deep knowledge of the Arabic language and his ability to use it were remarkable. Qutb's interpretation of the Quran – *Fi Zilal Al-Quran* ("In the Shadows of the Quran") – was an extraordinary work, but unfortunately it also promoted a lot of hatred and violence.

As with all jihadists, Zawahiri's ultimate goal was to recreate the Islamic Caliphate, that is, he sought to unite the Muslim world under a single leadership headed by a prince. This caliph would not merely provide spiritual leadership, but would actually govern the totality of Islamic dominions. It should be understood that Salafi Islam is political in its very essence, to the extent that it is fundamentally different in this regard from Judaism and Christianity. Judaism was forced to contend with the Diaspora at an early stage and learned to cooperate with host nations while preserving its religious identity. Similarly, when Christ was asked what deference should be given to temporal power, Christ responded with the well known maxim, "Render to Caesar the things that are Caesar's, and to God the things that are God's." In contrast to Christianity and Judaism, Salafi Islam teaches an aggressive military ideology designed to spread the religion and dominate the world.[11] Zawahiri, wished to dispense with the idea of the state, and individual states themselves. There would be one state, Islam, bound by Sharia law and ruled by the Caliph. For him, it was the world of Islam against the world of war (i.e. against the infidels), or in Arabic: *Dar al Islam* and *Dar al Harb*, respectively. In this sense, Zawahiri was not much different from many traditional scholars who taught the theoretical underpinnings of violence. It was not uncommon for a typical imam to rouse congregants in a prayer which cursed Jews and Christians. Zawahiri differed from them by teaching actual violence against our "enemies".

As we have witnessed time and again, this desire for a Caliphate puts Islamists on a collision course with the governments of any host country they reside in, in this case, Egypt. As it is written,

> *For they who do not judge in accordance with what God has bestowed from on high are, indeed, Infidels.*
> {Quran 5:44}

In other words, Zawahiri did not view the leaders of Islamic nations as true Muslims because, as *Jamaa Islamiya* interpreted it, they "do not rule by Islamic law." So it was that the Islamists not only objected to Sadat's peace with Israel

---

[11] Although Moses was powerful leader of the Hebrews and well cared-for by them, God forbade him to enter the land of Canaan.

and his goal of better ties with America, but they objected fundamentally to Egypt as a secular state and Sadat as a leader with temporal power.

Equally, Zawahiri decried the freedoms of the West as immoral weaknesses, as excesses, but also as threats. The West did not submit to Islamic law, yet it was both successful and powerful. He scorned the liberties of Western women, particularly their suggestive attire. Women, he believed, should be required by law to wear Islamic dress – at least the *hijab* and preferably the *niqab*. He envisioned a system similar to that implemented later by the Taliban, which compelled women to cover themselves.[12] If necessary, he believed it acceptable to indulge the freedoms of the West – but only as a vehicle for advancing the takeover of Islam.

Dr. Al-Zawahiri was faithful to his cause, but his spiritual identification became perverted. Islamist teachings twisted his religious fervor toward violence. He is certainly a leader of mass-murderers, but he is also a pawn of a perverted doctrine that warped him into a terrorist. I often wonder how Al-Zawahiri would have turned out if his childhood religious education had promoted love instead of hate and violence.

Second Thoughts

My entire relationship with *Jamaa Islamiya* lasted for approximately two to three years (from 1979-1982). It took about six months to become sufficiently indoctrinated. Over the next year, I became increasingly active in the movement. Eventually, my involvement reached the point where I thought myself prepared to train with jihadi groups in Afghanistan, to fight and kill in the name of Allah. It was at this time that my conscience began to awaken. I sensed I was

---

[12]It is an almost ubiquitous misconception that the burqa, worn by women in Taliban society, is the entire outfit. It is simply the portion of cloth that descends from the nose and covers
the neck.

on the wrong path. In the last eight months of membership I gradually withdrew.

One episode in particular gave me second thoughts. It transpired that I overheard a conversation between one Ahmed Omar and other members of the group. A fourth-year medical student, Ahmed was an "amir" of *Jamaa*. He was planning to kidnap a police officer and bury him alive. His exact word was *netaweeh*, which meant in Egyptian slang, 'to dig a grave for someone and bury him alive". The issue concerned a party that was planned that day at the medical school. Music and women singers were to be featured, and the view of *Jamaa* was, of course, that such an event was un-Islamic. Members of *Jamaa* gathered that day in thousands to protest the party and disrupt it by force. The police intervened and the medical school came under martial law.

It occurred to me then that the Quran doesn't actually forbid music. *Jamaa* and other Islamists base this prohibition not on Quranic verses, but on non-Quranic sources such as the Hadiths. There is a contradiction between the Quran and other approved Islamic books. But in thinking this way, I was doing the opposite of what *Jamaa* had taught me: I had started to analyze. The critical thinking with which my father had raised me helped me at the last moment. It ignited a spark that was to become a fire.

I recalled the time when I studied the Bible to debate the Christian students in high-school. In particular, I remembered the passage: *"For what shall it profit a man, if he shall gain the whole world, and lose his own soul?"* I pondered, "what if Islam was to subjugate the world, but lose its soul?" That early exposure to the Bible was crucial in helping me question violent aspects of Salafi teaching. Christ's statement played a pivotal role in giving me the moral fiber to swim against the stream of radical Islam, to resist it rather than appease it.

I remembered another verse from the Quran:

*O ye who believe! Stand out firmly for justice, as witnesses to God,
even as against yourselves, or your parents, or your kin.*
{Quran 4:135}

This time, I saw the meaning in a completely different light.
I understood it to mean that we should speak the truth even
if it conflicted with the common beliefs of one's culture. It
meant that we should say what we believe is good and useful
to all of mankind even if it violates the dictates of traditional
religious teachings.

I wondered, too, if the divine DNA molecule was "violent".
Does it attempt to conquer the rest of the cell? Does it try
to make the other cellular components like itself? It does
not. Rather, it cooperates and works harmoniously with its
neighbors to create and support life.

Finally, the existence of alternative forms of Islamic teaching
played a critical role in helping me to desist from the path
of jihad. Specifically, I was invited during this time to join a
very small sect of Islam that follows only the Quran. They
were known as Quranics and they rejected the Hadiths and
other Islamic texts. Consequently, members of this sect stood
against killing apostates, stoning women for adultery, and
killing gays. They viewed the early Islamic invasions as
immoral and senseless. The sect was not ideal – the respect
many followers had for Women's Rights was not very
satisfactory to me. Still, they were much less violent when
compared to Salafists, and they allowed me to think
critically, to approach the Quran in a non-traditional
manner. I was able to have different theologically-based
interpretations from those of other sect members without
mutual animosity. Tolerating different views was an
important creed of the Quranics. If this alternative sect had
not been available, it would have been much more difficult
for me to resist jihadism.

All these influences combined to cultivate in me a new
mentality that defied – and still defies – the violent
injunctions promoted by prevailing Islamic instruction.

Jamaa, of course, was not pleased. They tried to persuade me to return. We became embroiled in intricate debates about stoning women and secular rule which annoyed them greatly. They didn't threaten me with violence *per se*, but there were indirect threats ("Apostates such as you will be killed").

After I had left *Jamaa*, I began to preach a peaceful understanding of Islam. Once, I gave a sermon at a local mosque, and after prayers a gang of radical Muslims confronted me and my dear friend, Dr. Tarek Ragab. They punched him; then, as we ran from the mob, they pelted us with stones. Fortunately, we weren't significantly injured.

Final Remarks

It is vital that our educational systems teach young Muslims the value and skill of critical thinking. They must be exposed to other beliefs, cultures and religions and learn to respect them. Most importantly, the Islamic world must foster an alternative, theologically rigorous doctrine that rejects violence. All of these are necessary to modernize Islamic societies and decrease the likelihood of young Muslims turning to jihad.

The consequences of not learning the lessons have been dire and will continue to be so. By the late 1970s, Islamists had penetrated into every aspect of Egyptian life. They established competing banks which offered exceptionally high rates of return on deposits, sometimes 25%. As Egyptians gravitated to these banks, the result was a significant boost to the liquidity of Islamist coffers. In 1981, not long before I graduated, President Sadat was assassinated by a military lieutenant named Khaled Islambouli – a member of Islamic Jihad. The Iranians were delighted at the assassination and named a street after him. Zawahiri was also a member of Islamic Jihad, and was indicted for the assassination, but his connection to it was never proven. He was released from prison in 1984. Today, "Dr. Ayman" is the second-in-command of Al-Qaeda, and possibly its foremost leader.

The Muslim Brotherhood has met with as much "success", in some respects, as Al-Qaeda. Today, it is estimated that the Brotherhood controls 20% of the Egyptian parliament; some say 75% of the Egyptian electorate supports them. Not all of their support stems from Islamist constituents – a sizeable mass of voters simply believes that the Brotherhood is not corrupt and will restore both stability and economic prosperity.

Takfir Wa Al-Hijrra, among others, went on to slaughter many Egyptians and foreign tourists in Egypt. The "Blind Sheikh", Omar Abdel-Rahman was a spiritual leader of *Takfir*. Americans will recognize his name – he resides now in the US, in solitary confinement, for conspiring to blow up the United Nations building, New York city FBI branch, and for attempting to destroy the World Trade Centers in 1993 – a job finished by Al-Qaeda in 2001. Though estimates vary, it is thought that 75% of Al-Qaeda's top leadership is Egyptian. Of the 19 hijackers that day, 15 were Saudi Arabian and the rest hailed from other Arab countries; the leader – Muhammad Atta – was my countryman.

Chapter 2:

Myths and Misconceptions about Islamism

Chapter 2: Myths and Misconceptions about Islamism

Let's pause at this point and devote a chapter to the many myths that surround Islamic terror. If we do not address them now, they will distract us from our analysis later. Every medical doctor will assert that it is very difficult to treat a disease if it is misdiagnosed or if the disease is confused with the symptoms. If we misdiagnose, then we treat the wrong illness. If we confuse the roots of the illness or superficially mask its symptoms, we cannot effect a cure.

The same applies to the societal disease of terrorism. It is not an easy illness to face because it defies the dicta of commonly held political beliefs. Efforts have been made by many in the West to seek the "real" cause of the disease in every location but one: Islam as it is currently taught and practiced in the vast majority of communities.

In 2007, for example, United Nations Secretary General Ban Ki-Moon stated that the genocide in Darfur stems from global warming. He advanced the idea that the Janjaweed militias in Northern Sudan were exterminating the residents of Darfur because of drought (which–in his view–must be caused by global warming). Former President Jimmy Carter has gone one better by claiming, recently, that the deaths there of 450,000 non-Muslims is not "technically" genocide. And then there is CBS Terrorism Analyst and former CIA official Robert Scheuer, who not long ago compared Osama bin Laden to Stonewall Jackson (a Confederate general in the American Civil War) and maintained that the Islamist goal of a resurrected Caliphate is a canard "manufactured by Neoconservatives".

How did we get here?

To place the blame squarely on the practice of the world's second largest religion makes many uncomfortable (and puts a good number in danger, should they do so). Large Muslim communities reside in many nations and often constitute a powerful and vocal minority. Many analysts choose to ignore the fact that Islamic terrorism is primarily fueled by ideology – a solution seems unattainable when Islamist ideology permeates a religion of 1.5 billion adherents. In assuming other causes, however, these analysts acted like a doctor who assumed a fast-growing mass was benign because he didn't know how to treat it if it was cancerous.

Similarly, Western nations have many economic and strategic ties with Islamic states. Criticism of Islam and the Muslim community does not come without risk. The inclination is to excuse the religion as it is practiced and find some other reason for a scapegoat.

Fear is a big contributing factor. Western academicians and politicians want to appear tolerant at all costs – even to the point of tolerating an illiberal, intolerant ideology – because to appear intolerant is to appear unenlightened, even unintelligent. Peer pressure and political correctness weigh heavily, as do opportunities for promotion or election. Intolerance – at least as deemed so by the multicultural establishment – is an intellectual mark of shame. On the "street" level, citizens fear to ask pointed questions of their Muslim neighbors because of the civic disorder and violence they might expect to receive in reply.

Resentment, too, is a factor. There are those who believe that terrorists are "underdogs", that the position of terrorists reflects their own isolation, their sense of being outcast. They thus perceive jihadists to be "guys like themselves", down on their luck, kicking back at an "oppressive system".

Root Causes

There are indeed root causes of Islamic Terrorism. However, many root causes that have been proposed are misleading or wrong. Islamic terror in the view of many is the outcome of External Forces such as poverty, lack of education, Israel, US policies in the region, and so on. Some of these root causes arguments are easy to dispose of in their entirety; other root causes play a catalytic role, feeding into and fostering jihadism, but are not, by themselves, the true cause of it. All of them do, however, remain stubbornly popular. Let us examine them.

Poverty

A quick peek at the backgrounds of most Islamist leaders shows clearly and unmistakably that many, if not most of them, belong to a high socio-economic class. Bin Laden is a billionaire; Al-Zawahiri is the product of a wealthy family in Egypt. Many other Islamic terrorists, such as the home-grown terrorists in the UK, were from middle- and upper-class families. In addition, fifteen of the 9/11 hijackers were from Saudi Arabia, a country one can hardly consider poor. It is also true that most of the hijackers spent extensive time enjoying the affluence and privileges of American society; it didn't deter them from their mission at all. Were poverty the true cause of Islamic terrorism, we would have seen the majority of Islamic terrorists hail from a low socioeconomic class and from the poorest Islamic countries (Somalia, Bangladesh, etc.) rather than wealthy OPEC nations. One can easily note, also, that there are many nations and communities which are desperately poor but do not spawn terrorists. It would be difficult, for example, to point to statistically-significant numbers of terrorists from the ranks of Chinese rice farmers or from Mexico City's shantytowns.

In fact, many elements in the traditional Islamic ideology contribute to increased poverty. Oppression of women is one such example. Islamic countries lose a significant proportion of their potential Gross Domestic Product when 50% of their population is not sufficiently participating in the labor force. In Saudi Arabia, women are not allowed to drive cars. This creates excessive demand for taxi services and chauffeurs, so the country must hire foreigners to address the shortage of drivers. Moreover, when Islamic terrorists perpetrated the "Luxor Massacre" in 1992, Egypt's tourism industry collapsed almost totally. In other words, poverty increased because of Islamism. The latter concept can partially explain increasing poverty among the Palestinians in the West Bank and Gaza.

At issue, in this case, is not that terrorism has no relation to poverty, but that its role is one of facilitation. A vicious cycle is created in which jihadists find it easier to recruit new members when candidates suffer from poverty, after which these new recruits perpetrate acts of terror, which in turn creates more poverty. The figure below captures this cycle.

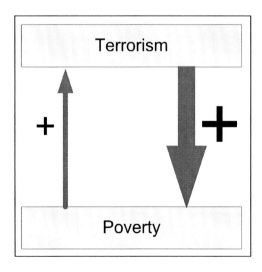

Figure 1 - The dynamic relationship between poverty and Islamic terrorism

In this model, terrorism and poverty work in a positive-feedback relationship. More importantly, one can observe that terrorism is the primary factor in this cycle while poverty is a secondary facilitator. It is vital to understand this mechanism precisely, because if we assess poverty to be the primary problem and not the secondary one, our efforts at combating terror will fail. We could, for example, authorize transfer payments to poor Islamic communities; doing so, however, will only result in funding Jihadists – they will use the money to finance weapons purchases and intensify their recruiting efforts. Although we must treat both the primary factor and the secondary ones, we do need to correctly identify that Islamism is the primary one.

When we see poor nations fail to produce terrorists but Islamic societies spawn them in large numbers, our diagram here should give us a clue: the more peaceful poor nations lack the ideology which generates the suicidal, terrorist mentality. Therefore, we must devote more of our resources to addressing jihadist ideology, the primary factor.

Discrimination

This root cause would have it that Islamic terrorism is a backlash against discrimination. It is held that Muslims are frustrated by inequality, injustice, and prejudice in their respective society, so a portion of them react to this perceived mistreatment by killing large numbers of innocents.

The problem with this "root cause" is twofold. On the one hand, it fails to explain why Muslims who do not experience discrimination become terrorists, and on the other, it does not explain why non-Muslims who are discriminated against do not become terrorists. It should be noted that not all Islamic terrorists are Middle Easterners – some are native Western converts to Islam. This leads to the subsidiary issue of whether such discrimination is more properly against Arabs, and if so, why non-Arab Muslims become terrorists and why non-Muslim Arabs in general do not become terrorists.

Of course, the existence of significant discrimination is itself questionable. According to 2006 FBI statistics, hate crimes against Muslims in the US are not especially frequent when compared to those against other religions, and against other groups. [13]

Table 1: FBI Hate Crime Statistics by Religion
(see appendix for full statistics: FBI Hate Crime Statistics)

Incidents, Offenses, Victims, and Known Offenders
by Bias Motivation, 2006

Bias motivation	Incidents	Offenses	Victims[1]	Known offenders[2]
Religion:	**1,462**	**1,597**	**1,750**	**705**
Anti-Jewish	967	1,027	1,144	362
Anti-Catholic	76	81	86	44
Anti-Protestant	59	62	65	35
Anti-Islamic	156	191	208	147
Anti-Other Religion	124	140	147	63
Anti-Multiple Religions, Group	73	88	92	49
Anti-Atheism/ Agnosticism/etc.	7	8	8	5

Yet, even if we were to grant the existence of discrimination against Muslims over-and-above that against other groups, it cannot explain why (e.g.) doctors in the UK – well paid, respected professionals – were involved in attempts to destroy transportation targets. It cannot also explain why Muslims in Arab countries commit acts of terror. For example, the Muslims who perpetrated the Luxor bombing in Egypt were Egyptians – do Egyptian Muslims face prejudice

---

[13]A nice find by Robert Spencer: US Department of Justice, Federal Bureau of Investigation, Criminal Justice Information Services Division, "2006 Hate Crime Statistics, Table 1", http://www.fbi.gov/ucr/hc2006/table1.html

in Egypt? Similarly, Jose Padilla was an American-born citizen, a non-Arab, but conspired to detonate a dirty bomb in Chicago's O'Hare airport. Azzam the American is another example of how an American-born convert to Islam became a member of an Islamic terror organization with aims of destroying his own country.

Lack of Education

Another frequently-cited "root cause" is the lack of education in Islamic societies. Again, Al-Zawahiri is a medical doctor. Bin Laden is highly-educated. One finds countless examples of educated terrorists.

Education can certainly play a very positive role in combating terror, provided it teaches peace, critical thinking, and real tolerance. But Salafist ideology, the most powerful force in mainstream Islamic education today, teaches virtually nothing of this kind. In fact, a more highly educated person is better able to absorb and spread the religious texts that promote brutality. In contrast, an illiterate person does not usually have the same opportunity to read and grasp Islamist writings and thus his understanding of the religion, in many situations, stops at the level of Islam's "Five Pillars". He may very well have a greater chance of maintaining his conscience unscathed, while the conscience of the educated person could be suppressed by violent religious indoctrination.

In the 1940s and 1950s, when Egypt had an illiteracy rate in excess of 90%, terrorism against tourists in the country was almost unheard-of. On the other hand, when literacy improved and people became better-able to assimilate Salafi Islamic theology, as indeed happened in the last few decades, killing innocent tourists has become a common phenomenon. Religious education can be beneficial if it teaches love, but if it teaches hate and intolerance, it can be catastrophic. Having knowledge or skills does not, by itself, make a person ethical or decent.

Absence of Democracy

One often hears today, particularly from the Western media and some Western politicians, that the source of Islamic terror in the Middle East is the absence of democracy. Yet this "root cause" is also plagued by counterexamples. If it is true, then what explains the phenomenon of "home grown" Jihadists in Western nations? The UK is certainly a democratic nation, and yet the perpetrators of the London subway attacks grew up in the UK. The British Muslims who became terrorists were not deprived of democracy. In contrast, Arab Christians – who not only live in un-democratic Arab societies but are actively persecuted in many of those societies – do not contribute to terrorism. Can "lack of democracy" truly be the "root cause" of the problem?

There are brave and noble individuals who fight for democracy in the Middle East. It is an essential and critical battle. But in their zeal to fight for democracy, many of these activists have led Western policymakers (of more than one political affiliation), to believe that lack of democracy is the "root cause" of Islamic terror. The idea resonated with many Western politicians both because it dovetailed with existing strategic goals, and because it seems, to many of them, that solving the problem of democracy is easier than addressing the malaise in traditional Islamic teaching. In this single respect, advocates for democracy have it backward. Islamism is an independent cause of terrorism. Democracy activists failed to perceive that Islamization can be a powerful and seductive force, perhaps because its barbarity is so fundamentally alien to them. We note with deep sorrow the assassination of Pakistan's Benazir Bhutto, and as my wife Maha has noted, it leads us to ask, if lack of democracy is the source of Islamic terror, then why did Jihadists there murder their best chance for it?

Democracy was granted to the Iraqi people. Millions voted, proudly so, for a wide range of candidates. Similarly, Arafat (after the Oslo accords) was widely hailed as a democratically-elected leader, in elections (many say, rigged) that were certified by former President Jimmy Carter. Both of these societies, under democratic political arrangements, have struggled with Islamism and Islamic terror. The conclusion can only be that democracy in the Middle East is not the magical solution to ending Islamic violence. In fact, what both these cases show is that when countries transition to democracy without due preparation, violence can reach almost uncontrollable levels.

Without question, democracy should be the ultimate strategic goal. Unfortunately, at the tactical level, defeating Islamism must take priority over the establishment of democracy. In the current climate where Islamist ideas dominate, democracy will simply encourage Islamists to "use democracy to end democracy". They will run as candidates, and when they achieve a majority, will shift to an authoritarian, Sharia-based government. In 1992 this actually happened in Algeria; Salafi groups led by Abbas Madany gained power in a democratic election and immediately declared the cessation of democratic government. Islamists are a parasite on democracy – they feed on a democratic host until the host perishes.

Western Colonialism and Imperialism

This "root cause" is a favorite of Western academics and Leftist intellectuals. As the argument goes, nations that were colonized or dominated by Western powers from the Age of Exploration to the first half of the 20th century harbor enormous resentment of these powers for injustices, many real and some mythical. Because Arab lands were victims of this colonialism, their lingering resentment fuels Islamic terror. Still others define colonialism loosely: claiming that Israel is a colony of the US, or that modern globalization of trade creates economic "colonies" out of developing nations. In the most fanciful definitions, Western cultural infusion itself constitutes imperialism, that is, jet planes, fast-food, suggestive attire, rock music, *et al* are "invading" traditional societies and violating their independence.

Israel, however, is a sovereign nation that has acted numerous times against the wishes of one or another US administration at various times in its history.[14] As for the "cultural" and globalization arguments, it cannot even loosely be imperialism because all countries have a choice whether to trade with foreigners or partake of foreign cultural offerings. The most common colonialist narrative that we encounter is that Arab nations are exploited by Western powers for their oil. This is an odd narrative, because the oil producing states required Western technology to extract the oil and invited foreign companies as partners, often granting them extensive drilling rights. By now, most OPEC nations have nationalized their oil industries – after they were established by Western companies. Petroleum has made Middle Eastern nations fabulously wealthy. In other words, we can safely dismiss these "loose" definitions.

Unfortunately for our proponents of "strict colonialism", Saudi Arabia – the largest exporter of Islamist terror – has never been colonized by the West. The holy Arabian *Hijaz* has been under consistent Muslim rule since the beginning of Islam. That is not to say that what we now call Saudi Arabia has never been colonized – simply, not by the West. Saudi Arabia's coastal strip along the Red Sea, which includes the holy cities of Mecca and Medina, was conquered and controlled by the Ottoman Turks, who were Muslim. Although Arabs on the whole were responsible for the lion's share of colonization in the Middle East, typically via holy war, non-Muslims in the region have rarely if ever been observed to detonate themselves, especially when citing Muslim colonization as their reason.

In general, the frequent and bloody wars between Muslims that we have seen throughout history serve in themselves to refute the "imperialism" root cause. It is hard to believe that

---

[14]The 1956 Suez Crisis is perhaps the most notable.

the brutal slaughter we see today of Muslims by Muslims has any relation to a Western occupation that ended decades ago, at least, for those countries that were actually occupied. Sunnis massacre Shias in Iraq for reasons other than colonialism. Western imperialism did not compel Algerian Muslims to decimate each other. Women in Islamic societies who failed to wear the *hijab* have had their faces burned by Islamists and are stoned for adultery. Gays are executed because their sexuality is considered immoral. Is anyone supposed to believe that these are the results of foreign occupation?

It remains also to explain why Hindus in India (colonized by the British for centuries) or Christians in Latin America have not pursued terror. Nor has the question been answered as to why Islamic terror manifested itself ubiquitously only after a significant spell of time had elapsed subsequent to foreign occupation. It would have been more consistent, had colonialism been the cause of jihadism, for terror to have started during or immediately after occupation. In fact, when Islamic nations were colonized, Sharia- and Islamism-based crimes were far less prevalent. Ironically, Islamic nations in many respects were more civilized under occupation than they are now; we virtually never heard of suicide bombings against tourists during that period.

We must be consistent. If we locate the cause of Jihadism in the historical colonization of the Middle East, then we should have the courage and intellectual integrity to blame the Islamic subjugation of the entire region at least as much as we admonish the West for it. In fact, the Western colonization of the Middle East – where it can be said to have occurred – did not change the language and the religion of the region's inhabitants. The Islamic conquests can lay no such claim; the Islamic invasions wiped out numerous preexisting religions and forced the Arabic language on the majority of the Middle East's inhabitants.

The Arab/Israeli Conflict

Here, the argument runs that the Arab/Israeli conflict creates resentment among the world's Muslims, who express their anger at Israel via terrorism. This "root cause" can be dismissed totally. The problem with the argument is that it fails to explain the global reach of jihad and the vast number of targets which have no relation to Israel. An estimated 200,000 Algerians perished in their civil war, where thousands of innocents were massacred, particularly by the Algerian Islamic Group, which was Salafist. Buddhists in Thailand have of late been experiencing a protracted campaign of Islamist terror. What do these examples of Islamic brutality have to do with Israel? There are countless other examples; in 2004, 1200 students were taken hostage by Jihadists in Beslan, Russia. Of these, 334 civilians perished and 108 schoolchildren were murdered, point-blank. Shia and Sunni murder each other in Iraq by the thousands, and here, too there is no connection to Israel. In fact, Sunni and Shia have been in violent conflict since the early caliphates, long before Israel's establishment.

Similarly, many readers may not remember that in 1991, more than 280,000 Palestinians were expelled from their homes. They had sided with Saddam Hussein during operation Desert Storm, and faced the consequences when his forces were defeated. The country that expelled them has experienced no world condemnation and very little terrorism. The expulsion has not been mentioned in Jihadist manifestos, and has never been cited as a motivation. The reason for the indifference is that the country which expelled them wasn't Israel. They were expelled from Kuwait – "Muslim brothers" of the Palestinians. If the predicament of the Palestinians was the source of global jihad, then one would expect that Kuwait would experience a protracted campaign of terror and that Muslims everywhere would attribute 9/11 to Kuwaiti expulsion of the Palestinians. Such an expectation would be mistaken.

Much more interesting than refuting this "root cause" is to try to explain its popularity. The argument is prevalent throughout the global media, and it saturates the halls of Academia. Blaming Israel is attractive to proponents of many competing, often conflicting, ideological positions, but most of all, blaming Israel is attractive because it is easy. As we have noted, criticism of Islam does not come without risk. There are 1.5 billion Muslims in the world today, and when, for example, cartoons of Muhammad were published in Denmark, there were riots across the globe. It is much easier to vent frustration at terrorism by scapegoating a tiny nation of Jews in conflict with a smaller nation of Palestinians, a combined population less than the city of Los Angeles. Fear and mental laziness, however, will not win a war on terror.

The role of oil in the national economies also plays a role. The OPEC nations are tremendously powerful. In combination, they possess an estimated 2/3 of the world's oil reserves and supply more than 41% of oil consumed today. Countries which depend on this oil are therefore reluctant to provoke diplomatic and economic crises with OPEC member nations by accurately placing the blame for Islamic terror where it belongs: on current Islamic teaching.

There are then a number of camps which have ulterior motives for demonizing Israel. Muslims, of course, prefer to point the finger at someone other than themselves. American and European neo-Nazis view the destruction of Israel as a positive development, and so find it convenient to both blame Israel for terrorism and apologize for Jihadists. It is a common theme on neo-Nazi websites to bitterly lament Islamophobia. American isolationist conservatives also have their reasons. They believe (wrongly) that American support of Israel constitutes a "foreign entanglement" that breeds resentment with no positive benefit. Finally, the international Left has its own motivations to blame Israel for Islamic terror.

In general, these posited "Root Causes" find favor in Leftist thought because it locates the source of the evil in external, material conditions. War – the Arab/Israeli conflict, in this case – creates Islamic terror, as their story goes, and not vice-versa. But there is more. A common Leftist template is that most of the world's problems stem from capitalist exploitation by imperialist nations. They continuously claim that problems in the developing world – civil war, poverty, starvation, genocide – are the vestiges of this exploitation. The problem for them is that Israel does not fit their template. It has allied itself with the West, particularly with the "Great Satan", the United States. It has utilized free markets and global trade and its close alliance with America to become a developed nation in less than 50 years. Israel is a counter-example to the conventional wisdom of External Conditions. Therefore, instead of hailing Israel as an example of liberal democracy in a geopolitical region where it is almost never to be found, instead of defending a small nation bullied and attacked by oil-rich Islamic nations, the international Left has chosen to demonize Israel as an oppressor of the Palestinians, and locate global Islamic terror in the conflict. The international Left is overwhelmingly, almost entirely, anti-American, and for this reason alone there is animus toward Israel for its friendship and alliance with America.

It should be noted that bin Laden himself has named the Arab/Israeli conflict as a reason for his actions. However, bin Laden has also listed a wide variety of motives. His first video after 9/11 did not name Israel, but cited the presence of American military bases on Saudi soil as the impetus for the attack on the twin towers. Both of these reasons, however, are tactical obfuscations borrowed, it seems, from these Leftist talking points. His real motivation is to subjugate the world to Islam – a goal supported by statements of jihadists everywhere and on every level.

US Foreign Policy

It is commonly heard, conventional wisdom that US foreign policy in the Middle East is at the root of Islamic terror.

Certainly, there have been mistakes in US policy, but this cannot be the cause of Islamism. It goes without saying that no country's foreign policy is immune to mistakes, and if the policies of non-Islamic nations were the source of Islamism, then it cannot explain why American policy is singled-out. In fact, it was America that financed the Mujahidin resistance to the Soviet invasion of Afghanistan. Why, then, doesn't bin Laden thank the US for its support in that war and why does he not harbor any special animus toward Russia? Why doesn't the Left admonish Soviet imperialism?

The reason for jihadist animosity to America is that they seek superiority for Islam. This is based on their interpretation of the following Quranic verse:

> *It is He who hath sent His Messenger with guidance and the Religion of Truth, to proclaim it over all religion, even though the Pagans may detest (it).*
> {Quran 9:33}

Jihadists would not be able to exult as much in Islamic superiority if they defeated countries like Russia or China, because those countries are not the most powerful. On the other hand, defeating the US, which is the most powerful, will give them that feeling of elation. Furthermore, jihadists know that (e.g.) the Chinese government would most likely respond to terrorism severely, so that the negative impact of defeat on the Islamic image would be too great a risk. In contrast, jihadists know that American concern for human rights constrains retaliation and also blunts its wrath at the Muslim community.

More importantly, American involvement in the Middle East has been, on the whole, positive. One almost never hears about these positive contributions, never finds them cited in balance to criticisms, or sees it pointed out that other nations haven't made the same extensive contributions. The US assisted the economic and infrastructural development of many Islamic nations. Prior to nationalization, Standard Oil explored and drilled Saudi oil fields and built a large number of their refineries. Americans have consumed and still consume a great deal of that oil. It has afforded the Saudis and other OPEC nations a luxurious lifestyle. Dubai, for example, has become a beautiful and desirable destination to live and work, and US investments played a key role in that development. Were these US policies wrong? Considering Islam as a whole, why does America earn no points for saving the Muslims in Bosnia?

If America was truly an imperialist nation it would have simply conquered and obliterated the OPEC nations. It has had the military capability to do so for decades. On the contrary, America has spent billions on its current effort to establish democracy in Iraq – to win "hearts and minds" – and has reaped, as of this writing, no financial reward. Indeed, the Iraq War itself is frequently touted as a motivation for jihadists. But there was Islamic terror long before the current war in Iraq, and long before the first Iraq War, "Desert Storm". It should be noted that "Desert Storm", in 1990, utilized a coalition that included Arab nations, yet jihadists rarely blame those Arab nations for it, or attack them.

It is true that some citizens of the wealthy Arab nations suffer from poverty and mistreatment, but that is the result of internal corruption and Islamism. To place the primary blame for Islamic terror on American foreign policy is therefore illogical and unfair.

The Meaning of "Jihad"

Apologists for jihadism frequently claim that the true meaning of the word "jihad" is unconnected with violence. Typically, one hears that it means "peaceful struggle" or "defensive struggle". The non-violent interpretation is often advanced by Muslims to avoid criticism of Islam, especially after 9/11.

It is a simple fact that the violent meaning of "jihad" is the prevailing one in mainstream Islamic writing. If "jihad" was commonly understood to be peaceful, we would find Islamic charities and advocacy groups utilizing the word in their titles. But one virtually never hears of a peaceful Islamic organization that uses "jihad" in its name, while in contrast, "jihad" is commonly found in the titles of Islamic terror groups. We have already mentioned the Egyptian *al-Jihad* and the Palestinian group by the same name, and there are many more: for example, *Jama'at al-Jihad al-Islami* (Al-Qaeda affiliate active in central Asia), *Jihad Rite* (Australia), *Laskar Jihad* (Indonesia), and even a Turkish Islamic Jihad. Most people do not know that a less common name for Al-Qaeda is *Qa'idat al-Jihad*, and that the group we commonly hear reported as "Al-Qaeda in Iraq" goes by the formal name, *Tanzim Qaidat al-Jihad fi Bilad al-Rafidayn*.

Technically, "jihad" has at least five different meanings. Some of them are peaceful and others quite violent. In the strict, literal sense, "jihad" means to struggle or to resist something that pressures or oppresses. According to the Salafi interpretation, "jihad" means to either defend the Muslim community from an enemy or to convert non-Muslims by holy war. The latter understanding was the theological justification that early Muslims utilized to subjugate neighboring nations, and it is also the one unanimously endorsed by the main four Islamic jurisprudence schools (*madhab*): Maliki, Hanhbali, Shafeii, and Hanafi. It flourishes unchallenged in mainstream Islamic texts (such as *Fiqh Al-Sunna* and *Minhaj al-Muslim*).

The Sufi branch of Islam usually understands "jihad" as "internal struggle", that is, to resist the evil ideas and desires within oneself. This view derives from a hadith of Prophet Muhammad. After one of his raids, Muhammad said to his disciples:

We have returned from the smaller jihad to the bigger jihad... the disciples of Muhammad said to him: what is the greater jihad then he said "Jihad Al-Nafs" which means internal struggle against evil thoughts and human fleshly desires.
Al-Baihaqi and Al-Khateeb

However, this excellent understanding of the word "jihad" is not the dominant one in our Mosques and the Islamic education system. If you asked a young Muslim child in the Arab world to define "jihad", in most cases the answer will be, "War against the Infidels".

The small Quranic sect to which I belonged viewed jihad as preaching the Quran only by the word rather than the sword. Their view is grounded in the following verse:

Fight them (do your jihad) by preaching the Quran.
{Quran 25:52}

There is also a meaning of "jihad" that has been used in the Quran but is uncommon in traditional Islamic instruction: to struggle in search of God by studying his miracles in nature. This very rare understanding is based on the following verse:

And those who strive in our (cause) - We will certainly guide them to our Paths: For verily Allah is with those who do right.[15]
{Quran 29:69}

In the preceding passage, a derivative of the word "jihad" – *jahadu* – is employed to mean "strive in our case". In short, jihad can certainly be understood in a non-violent manner, but the dominant sense in most mainstream Islamic books is violent. A new interpretation of Islamic texts which utilizes peaceful meanings of "jihad" will benefit Islamic instruction and improve our security, but it is misleading and dishonest to claim that the non-violent understanding is in any way typical today.

---

[15]In both these two verses (25:52 and 29:69) the word jihad is used in the Arabic text of the Quran but in different derivatives (Respectively, *jahidhum* and *jahadu*).

"Jihadists just want to be heroes"

Some have suggested that the motivation for Muslims to commit acts of terror lies in their desire to be heroic. For example, in an interview on The World Today [10/3/2007 12:21], Dr. Marc Sageman stated that new jihadists "don't know much about Islam, but they just want to be heroes". Ultimately, the "hero worship" analysis dangerously minimizes the role of Islamist ideology. The problem with such an analysis lies in two areas: overemphasis of secondary factors, and methodology.

The desire of a person to be a hero, and to be admired by his community, is not unique to Muslims. Individuals all over the world, from every culture, every geographic location, every economic background and every religion seek to be heroes. In itself, the desire to be a hero is not even a bad thing – it is in many respects a virtue. A person might wish to save lives and so become a doctor, or might wish to defend his country by serving in the military. A man or woman might strive to be a star tennis player or campaign heroically to stop toxic pollution. But when large numbers of Muslims commit acts of terror to be heroes, and the community lauds them for it or does nothing, the problem is not the desire to be a hero, but a cultural and ideological disease in the community as a whole. If the Muslim community cultivates these jihadists, praises them, and sanctions or dismisses the problem, we must focus chiefly on the community and much less on a member's desire to please it.

Take the case of two brothers, as often happens, both Muslim, both exposed to the same Islamist indoctrination. One has a greater desire to be a hero, the other less so. Normally, neither would become a terrorist; but when we introduce Islamism, one becomes a suicide bomber, while the other does not take the final step. The solution in this case is to remove the Islamism, not the heroism. It is impossible, and not even necessarily desirable to smother a young Muslim's desire to be praised and recognized by his community, provided that the community praises the right behavior. It is similarly very difficult, if not impossible, to determine a person's psychological proclivity toward heroism. It is possible, on the other hand, to defeat the Islamist ideology.

Salafi ideology, in other words, is what may be called the "activating agent". To understand this better, let us resort to a medical metaphor. Imagine two cells in the human body. One cell might have a predisposition to become cancerous and the other is normal. Both cells, however, do not develop cancer until a carcinogenic chemical is introduced to the body. When that happens, the one with the predisposition becomes cancerous. The medical treatment solution is not to eliminate all cells with a predisposition, which is currently impossible, but to eliminate the carcinogenic chemical. So it is the case with jihadism. We must eliminate the cancerous ideology of Islamism – not combat the predisposition for a young men to be heroes. It may be the case, as well, that every cell in person's body has a predisposition to cancer. Proponents of the "hero" analysis, by logical extension, would necessarily assert that the whole body should be destroyed, even though the person can only acquire cancer by exposure to the chemical. Thus, the suggestion of Dr. Sageman to provide Muslims with different models of heroism could be helpful, but by itself it is not enough to eradicate jihadism.

Another problem with the "hero" analysis is that it fails to explain the division of labor among members of a terrorist group. Ayman al-Zawahiri has not yet detonated himself on a bus or in a pizza parlor, and is unlikely to ever do so. He directs other young Muslims to perform these deeds. Similarly, does the person who funds the terror, arranges fake passports, drives bombers to the target – who never becomes famous or is even heard of – does he participate because he wants to be a hero? If terrorism derives from a quest for personal glory, what explains the motives of those in a terrorist group who devotedly and anonymously perform the drudgery?

Furthermore, in the same interview about terrorism, Dr. Sageman also stated, "Right now what's fuelling it is a sense of moral outrage that young Muslims see in terms of Iraq". Unfortunately, the "hero" theory – in the absence of an ideological component – does not explain why Arab Christians, suffering from identical pressures of war in Iraq, are not interested in becoming "heroes" while their fellow Muslims are. Suicide bombing inside and outside Iraq is almost always conducted by Muslims rather than Christians.

"Al-Qaeda resembles the IRA"

It has been continuously fashionable among many Western writers to treat all forms of terrorism as broadly being the same. These pundits never fail to draw comparisons between Islamic terrorist organizations and other terrorist groups, such as the Irish Republican Army. In a 2005 editorial in the UK's Guardian, religion-writer Karen Armstrong opined that "Islamic terror" was an inadequate and unfair phrase for Islamic terror.

> *We rarely, if ever, called the IRA bombings "Catholic" terrorism because we knew enough to realise that this was not essentially a religious campaign. Indeed, like the Irish republican movement, many fundamentalist movements worldwide are simply new forms of nationalism in a highly unorthodox religious guise. This is obviously the case with Zionist fundamentalism in Israel and the fervently patriotic Christian right in the US.[16]*

As to her poor comparison of Islamism with "Zionist fundamentalism" and the American Christian right, we address this topic in a later chapter. As regards the IRA, it is true that "Catholic terror" is an incorrect description of IRA bombings. However, Armstrong is grossly mistaken to say

---

[16]Karen Armstrong, "The label of Catholic terror was never used about the IRA", *Guardian Unlimited*, July 11, 2005, http://www.guardian.co.uk/comment/story/0,3604,1525714,00.html

that "Islamic terror" inaccurately describes terror perpetrated by jihadists. Why?

If it were correct to use the phrase "Catholic terror", it would imply that Catholics across the globe – from the Middle East to Europe to America to Indonesia – commit terrorist acts. It would imply that Catholic communities everywhere have large contingencies of terror supporters. It would mean that Catholics murder Buddhists in Thailand, or blow up night clubs in Bali, or detonate themselves on Israeli school buses, or fly planes into skyscrapers. If Catholics were to engage in these types of attacks around the globe, with wide community support, we would be justified in calling it "Catholic terror"; but because Catholics have not done so, except in Ireland and the UK, we correctly refrain from using the phrase "Catholic terror". Indeed it is true, that although members of the IRA happened to have been Catholic, the goal of their terror had limited focus. Their complaints were irredentist and national. Had the English settlers in Northern Ireland been Catholic instead of Protestant, it is hard to believe that the conflict in Ireland would not exist.

Where Armstrong and others err is to assume Islamic terrorism is similar to terrorism by non-Islamic groups. In reality, Islamic terror is being perpetrated on a daily basis, worldwide. Large numbers of Muslims in places as disparate as America and Thailand support, finance, and take pride in terrorist acts by their fellow Muslims. Millions more are silent in the face of the carnage perpetrated by their own people. Equally as important, Islamic terrorist organizations refer to themselves in Islamic terms. The IRA never referred to itself as the "Catholic Republican Army". In contrast, Islamic Jihad and *Jamaa Islamiya* are just two examples of Islamic terrorist groups that use "Islam" in their names. They do not call themselves "Egyptian Jihad", or the "Egyptian Brotherhood" instead of the Muslim Brotherhood. Finally, and most critically, Islamic terrorist groups indoctrinate young Muslims with Islamic writings and Islamist ideology.

Clearly, it is entirely accurate to refer to Islamic terror as "Islamic terror"; what is more, it is inaccurate and dangerous to draw simplistic and ignorant comparisons between Islamic terror and other forms of terror. The goals of the IRA were narrow in focus; conflict in Ireland has died down considerably from political concessions and police actions. If we were to apply the same strategies to Islamic terror, we would utterly fail to stop it, and worse, we would jeopardize modern, democratic societies. Islamists care nothing for national boundaries; Al-Qaeda will not be satisfied with turning one country into a Taliban-style nation of misery. Islamic terror seeks to subjugate the entire non-Muslim world to Islam, by force. It sees the world as its battleground and the stakes as universal.

Chapter 3:

The Failure of Islamic Societies

Chapter 3: The Failure of Islamic Societies

Background: Sufi and Salafi

To the vast majority of people, the attacks of September 11, 2001 came as a surprise. Days, weeks or even months would pass for most people without once thinking of Islamic terror. It was a minor inconvenience that occurred in distant, hopeless lands, motivated by obscure passions and unfathomable complaints. Sheikh Abdul Rahman's attempt to bring down the Twin Towers in 1993 seemed an amateurish Islamist side-note to the nascent digital revolution, itself about to explode. September 11 spawned the same question in the mind of every citizen: what mysterious society could produce this latest savagery? Unlike the bombing of Pearl Harbor, the perpetrator was not a country. Nor was it the anomalous product of an isolated, deranged individual, as was the case with Timothy McVeigh. The words "Islamism", "jihad", and "Wahabbi" appeared on people's lips. Dozens of experts weighed in, some insightfully, others less so, and countless expositions were published, some illuminating, many profoundly misguided.

To make some sense of Islamic terror, a non-Muslim citizen must find a way to digest categories of Islamic belief into a bird's eye view that is both accurate and practical. Citizens must ultimately make decisions for their country and their communities; it will not suffice to be intimidated by some experts who often disguise very dubious conclusions and ideological agendas in a fog of irrelevant or exaggerated details.

So then, what are the main Islamic forces at play? Immediately, those who watch the daily violence on the evening news will volunteer, "Sunni and Shia". It may come as a surprise, but Sunni and Shia do not differ doctrinally in very interesting ways. Their conflict is largely sectarian, stemming from the early Caliphates. The Sunnis asserted, at least superficially, that Islam has no favorites among believers, and therefore any Muslim is technically entitled to be Caliph. The Shia insisted that the Caliphate must be headed by a descendent of Muhammad and offered, in turn, their candidate. Over this dispute, battle was joined at Karbala in 680 CE, where the Shia side was massacred. Since then, many Sunni regard Shia as false Muslims, and the Shia sect enshrines their loss at Karbala into a victimized ethos of the disinherited. In other words, the difference between the two hardly resembles the deep theological differences between Protestant and Catholic Christianity.

This is not to say that the conflict between Sunni and Shia is not important. On the contrary, in terms of human rights concerns as well as geopolitical decision-making, the Sunni-Shia divide is of utmost importance. However, it plays less of a role in terms of global Islamic terrorism; there are Sunni terrorist groups, and less frequently, Shia terrorist groups. There are Sunni terrorist regimes (Hamas) and terror-sponsoring Shia states (Iran). Terror organizations are motivated by most of the same objectives, utilize largely identical tactics, and most importantly, are sworn enemies of Western liberal values. Therefore, it is much better, for our purposes, to speak of Islam in terms of *Sufi* and *Salafi*.

Salafi Islam, or Salafism, corresponds closely to what may be called Fundamentalist Islam. It was in earlier times most prevalent in the holy Arabian Peninsula, known as the *hijaz*. Sufi Islam, or Sufism, is loosely speaking, a spiritual version that, in the past at least, encompassed more-or-less the rest of the Islamic dominions. In the modern era, we can also speak of Secular Islam or Liberal Islam.

Sufi Islam

Sufi Islam emphasizes mysticism and a personal relationship with the Creator. It might be characterized as a "mixed" form of Islam: some suggest that its early influences included Hindu and Buddhist currents, as well as shamanic elements from Central Asia. Members sometimes utilize trancelike meditation – accomplished by repetition of Quranic verses – to bring about communion with the creator. The sect has a number of mainstream and non-mainstream orders, as well as a variety of past and present "Masters", or luminaries, who have contributed many spiritual innovations. Sufism permits art and music to flourish. Perhaps the most famous examples of Sufis (although by far not the most prevalent) were the "Whirling Dervishes", who would dance or "whirl" to music to achieve ecstatic, transcendent states. Sufi Muslims often visit shrines where virtuous individuals are buried. These are known as *Awleiiaa Allah Al-Saleheen*, or the "Righteous People of Allah", whom Sufis ask for blessings.

There are no reliable statistics on the total number of Sufis, but they certainly number in the millions. Moreover, many Muslims share elements of Sufism and Salafism simultaneously which makes it difficult to estimate the world's Sufi population.

Sufism, then, is relatively peaceful (but not entirely). It typically considers jihad as an internal struggle against the individual's evil inclinations. Jews and Christians were able to survive under Sufi governance. In fact, as Bernard Lewis has pointed out, Christian dissenters and Jews sometimes found existence to be more tolerable under these Sufi-influenced Islamic societies than in Medieval Christendom. However, we must note the word "survive". Technically, traditional Islamic teaching permits non-Muslims to reside in the Islamic community, but only as Dhimmis, or second-class citizens. Dhimmis are forced to pay a humiliating poll-tax (*jizya*), but they otherwise need not be molested. Thus, in some Islamic areas Jews and Christians thrived at various times. Under the Egyptian Mamluks and Turkish Ottomans, for example, some Jews even became viziers ("consuls") to the Caliph or Sultan. Tolerance within Sufism is exemplified by the following poem.

O Marvel! A garden amidst the flames.
My heart has become capable of every form:
It is a pasture for gazelles and a convent for Christian monks,
and a temple for idols and the pilgrim's Kaa'ba,
and the tables of the Torah and the book of the Quran.
I follow the religion of Love: whatever way Love's camels take,
that is my religion and my faith.
>   Ibn al-Arabi, Tarjuman al-Ashwaq,
>   from *The Mystics of Islam*, translated by Reynold A. Nicholson

This poem was written by Muhammad Ibn Ali Ibn Arabi (1165 - 1240 AD) known as *Muhyiddin* ("Reviver of Religion") and *Shaykh al-Akbar* ("Greatest Master"). He was born into the Moorish culture of Andalusian Spain and traveled widely in the Islamic world.

Salafi Islam

While Sufism is a true branch of Islam, Salafism, in contrast, is not precisely a discrete sect or a formal organization. It is more of a force, a powerful reactionary energy that can impose itself on any Islamic society or group. Very few Muslims would identify themselves or think of themselves as "Salafist". Many Muslims who are in every respect Salafist would not even know the term. An adequate English approximation for "Salafi" would be "Fundamentalist".

Salafism seeks a return to the envisioned purity and perfection of early Islamic times. It strives for a literal interpretation of the Quran and holds the early leaders of Islam as examples for believers; the Arabic word *salaf* means "ancestors". Salafists base their doctrine on one of Muhammad's Hadiths:

> *The people of my generation are the best, then those who follow them,*
> *and then those who follow the latter.*
>   Sahih Muslim

Prophet Muhammad, naturally, is the best role model, and Salafists seek to emulate his behavior as closely as possible, most notably in dress and table manners, but also in his warlike zeal (as described in traditional Islamic writings). Bin Laden, for example, sits on the ground to dine, eats with his right hand (even though he is left handed), and dresses in a style that fits Sunna models as taught by Salafists.

Salafists insist that Islam has gradually been diluted with sensuality and worldly indulgence, a sinful departure from the religion's austere roots. Utilizing the Quranic verses, and particularly the hadiths, Salafism places strict limitations on the rights and behavior of women. It restricts art, especially the visual arts and music. And these restrictions are enforced by violence and barbaric punishments spelled-out in doctrine. Salafists desire a return to the Islamic Caliphate. They do not respect secular states or weakly Islamic regimes. They believe that Sharia Law should constitute, ideally, the only legal system in any society because it is the Divine Law. Here is an archetypical passage employed by Salafists:

> According to Ibn Abbas, Prophet Muhammad had said: "The most essential fundamentals of Islam are three. If someone did not apply any of them he should be considered an Infidel and his blood is Halal (it is acceptable to kill him) These three foundations are: Saying no God except Allah and Muhammad is the prophet of Allah, praying the five prayers (every day), and fasting of Ramadan"
> Abu Yaali with Good narration
> Fikh allsunna: Prayer chapter

As we see, Salafism can create hard-hearted individuals who accept ruthless conduct. It suppresses a Muslim's conscience while making him feel he is devout.

Since 9/11, we have heard that the *Wahabbi* sect in Saudi Arabia has been exporting terror, and we similarly heard the word "Wahabbism". What is the relation of *Wahabbi* to *Salafi*? The answer is quite simple: Wahabbism is a concrete manifestation of Salafism. In other words, the Wahabbis apply existing Salafi doctrine; they never invented new theology. The sect was founded in Saudi Arabia by Muhammad Ibn Abd al-Wahhab (1703–1792). Wahabbists reject visiting shrines (except for the grave of Muhammad), and consider such behavior to be idolatrous. For this reason, Ibn Abd al-Wahhab destroyed all the shrines in Saudi Arabia, but left Muhammad's intact. Muhammad's grave is customarily visited by pilgrims during the *haj*.

Wahabbism, then, is the prevailing Islamic force in Saudi Arabia, and it furnishes us with an important example of Salafism. Women there are forced to completely cover-up their faces with a black mask known as the *niqab*. Muslims are required by law to attend prayer five times per day. It is strictly forbidden to build Christian churches in Saudi Arabia. It is, indeed, a nation of religious apartheid. In Mecca, there are separate freeways for Muslims and non-Muslims. People are beheaded for crimes such as adultery, homosexuality, and converting from Islam. Lesser crimes, such as theft, meet with amputation of limbs. The national flag of Saudi Arabia features the scimitar and the words, "No God except Allah and Muhammad is the prophet of Allah". This sentence is a required utterance for a person converting to Islam. The words are regularly cited as justification to subjugate and subdue non-Muslims, who are given the option to convert, pay the humiliating *jizia* tax, or be killed.

One of the most prominent Salafi scholars in Saudi Arabia is Sheikh Saleh Al-Fawzan. He is the author of the religious textbook, *Al-Tawhid* ("Monotheism"), which is not only used to teach Saudi high school students, but their Western and non-Western counterparts abroad. In recent years, Fawzan declared: "slavery is a part of Islam" and also, "slavery is part of jihad, and jihad will remain as long as there is Islam." Fawzan insisted that those who promote the view that Islam can exist without slavery are "ignorant", indeed, "infidels", and added that they are not scholars, but merely writers.[17] By declaring that Muslims who reject slavery are infidels, he is declaring them to be apostates. The portion of

[17]Daniel Pipes, comment on "Saudi Religious Leader Calls for Slavery's Legalization", *Daniel Pipes' Weblog*, comment posted November 7, 2003, http://www.danielpipes.org/blog/123

Sharia concerned with apostates is known as *Redda* law, and according to the literal implementation of *Redda* in Saudi Arabia, the punishment for apostasy is death. In other words, Fawzan has declared that Muslims who reject slavery in Islam should be killed.

Sheikh Fawzan is hardly a fringe radical. He is a member of Saudi Arabia's Senior Council of Clerics – their highest religious body. He serves on their Council of Religious Edicts and Research. He is also the Imam of the Prince Mitaeb Mosque in Riyadh, and if that is not enough, a professor at Imam Muhammad Bin Saud Islamic University, the main Wahabbi center of learning.[18] For Salafists, the perfect world is one in which apostates are slain, adulterous women are stoned to death, and enslavement of war captives is permitted. Polygamy is admired and wives can be beaten when the husband deems it appropriate.

Salafism is intimately connected with violence. In some cases, terror and brutality are actually perpetrated, as with jihadist groups. These groups adhere to the concept of *Al-Takfeer Wa Al-Istihlal*, which allows them to consider non-members of their organization as infidels. It explains why they show little compunction in killing fellow Muslims. A good example of a Salafist groups which follow *takfeer* were those in Algeria, who exterminated 200,000 Muslim innocents and burnt the faces of many Muslim women for refusing to wear the *hijab*. Many Salafists believe that violent jihad is the solution for most of the problems in the Muslim world. They look to the early successes of the Islamic conquest, when Muslims declared wars on the infidel, won these wars, and established an empire.

As we have mentioned, Jews and Christians could normally survive and sometimes flourish under Sufi-influenced rule. The same cannot be said for Salafi Islam in the Arabian Peninsula, from whence Jews and Christians were evicted. We see the outcome today: one is hard-pressed to find even

---

[18]Ibid.

a single Saudi Jew or Saudi Christian. True enough, Jews were also expelled from Egypt under the Nasser regime, but that expulsion was political rather than religious, and in any event, Egypt still harbors communities of Jews and Christians. In contrast, the whole Saudi nation has been ethnically and spiritually cleansed by the Salafi Islamic sword.

Secular Islam

For completeness' sake we must mention one other force in the Islamic demographic: Secular Islam.

Secular Islam is an expression predominantly used in the West to describe what is perceived as liberal Muslims. Broadly speaking, secular Muslims apply various elements of the Muslim culture rather than following a text-based belief system. They may apply culturally-transmitted Islamic moral codes but do not study the texts. Like Sufis, secular Muslims may be influenced by surrounding non-Islamic cultures, e.g., Judeo-Christian traditions in the Middle East or Hindu and Buddhist cultures in parts of Asia. These cultural infusions have resulted in the passive rejection of some Salafist tenets. Polygamy, for example, is relatively unacceptable in Egypt but much more tolerated in Wahabbi-dominated Saudi Arabia. Polygamy is less common in Egypt because Egyptian Muslims have lived alongside Jews and Christians who do not practice it.

Finally, there are also Muslims who do not fit easily into any of these Muslim categories, since they represent a variable mix of all combined groups. Some may put on a moderate façade while their minds are primarily influenced by Salafi elements.

Salafism Explodes

Wahabbis Become Wealthy

As we have seen, the Wahabbis have been active in the Saudi peninsula since the 18th century. It is only in the last several decades, however, that they have become a global force. This has happened because the sect acquired access to the flood of petrodollars flowing into Saudi coffers. The effect of Wahabbi wealth has operated on three levels. First, when the Saudis became wealthy, they were widely admired in the Islamic world. Muslims elsewhere wondered why the Saudis should be so blessed, and attention turned to their Salafist religious practice. Muslims in less wealthy states reasoned that they, too, would be blessed if they adopted Salafist beliefs. Relatively moderate implementations of Islam began to be pushed aside to make way for Salafi doctrine. Second, the flourishing Saudi economy required skilled labor and outside expertise. To fill the void, numerous non-Saudi Muslims traveled there to work. They were exposed constantly to the overpowering Wahabbi influence in their daily life, so that many of these foreign workers returned to their home countries more Islamized. Most of these workers became wealthy by the standards of their societies, which helped consolidate the perception that adherence to Salafi teaching brings blessings and wealth to its followers. These workers often supported Salafism in their local, home communities by financing Salafi institutes and charities. Third, and most importantly, the Wahabbis utilized their new wealth to fund the propagation abroad of their Salafist version of Islam. They continue to finance Salafi mosques in countless locations overseas and have made their literature available, at little cost, to Muslims around the world.

Relatively moderate Islam lost ground in societies everywhere. "Moderate", in the sense that Jews and Christians were not eradicated from these non-Saudi states. "Relatively", because the Islam taught outside of Saudi

Arabia still considers non-Muslims to be second-class citizens, or *ahl al-dhimma*.

Jihad: Umma to Individual

Salafi ideology presented weakly Islamic or secular Arabist regimes with a dilemma. A growing percentage of their home populations subscribed to a doctrine that categorically rejected the nation-state itself, did not respect temporal power and sought to replace it with Sharia. On the other hand, if the regime were to crush Salafi adherents and their groups, it would appear barbaric to many of its own citizens as well as those in the Western world who defend freedom of religion. Faced with this predicament, regimes compromised. They granted Salafists some freedom to organize and espouse their beliefs as long as they did not threaten the government. In addition, not a few regimes found Salafists could be useful despite the danger they posed. Salafists could, for example, be given room to destroy political opponents; in the case of Egypt, some claim that Sadat used them against the Nasserists.

Yet while Arab regimes granted Salafists some freedom to practice, governments still limited their activities. Salafists therefore sought a strategy to defeat these regimes – a strategy that would also be essential to global Islamic conquest – and they found it. The solution was to transfer – via reinterpretation of doctrine – the responsibility of violent jihad from the Islamic collective, or *Umma*, to the individual Muslim.

Traditionally, the responsibility to declare war on the infidel rested with the Umma. This is the mainstream interpretation of Islamic law and all Islamic schools of jurisprudence have, in the past, supported this understanding. In the last 50 years this interpretation has changed. By shifting the level of jihad to the individual, every Muslim became obliged to share in it and help re-establish the Islamic Caliphate. He should not, indeed must not, wait for collective bodies to give him the "green light". This 'individualization' of jihad was based on the following Quranic verse:

> *Then fight in Allah's cause – You are held responsible only for yourself – and rouse the believers (to fight).*
> {Quran 4:84}

The transfer of responsibility could not have been achieved without the backing of theological rigor. It became a topic of debate whether Muslims should wait for the re-establishment of the Caliphate to declare war on the Infidels, or should personally undertake the battle at once. I witnessed these doctrinal disputes between various members and leaders of *Jamaa Islamiya*, as well as in numerous mosques.

It may seem that a narrow doctrinal shift of this type could not be significant. In fact, it was critically important. It provided the theological justification that enabled the small-group Islamic terrorism we have seen in recent years. An already barbaric concept was energized by a new, aggressive focus. Among many others, Ayman al-Zawahiri was its champion.

Passive Terrorism

The seeds of Islamic Terror could not have sprouted into a flourishing weed if they did not find fertile soil in which to germinate. Such soil can be found in the world's Muslim community. A large percentage of the Muslims today passively approve of Islamic terror, or do nothing about it, or minimize it, or shift the blame. Some of these behaviors are deliberate strategies by Islamists to support actual terrorists by misleading their pursuers. In other cases, it is an unconscious unwillingness to face the problem. Therefore, the term "passive terrorism" refers to a broad category of enabling behaviors and beliefs, both calculated and uncalculated, which serve to exacerbate jihadism.

Passive Support

For every jihadist in the world there are a much larger number of individuals who quietly approve of his conduct. Islamic terror often makes passive terrorists secretly proud. The relationship of passive terrorism to active terrorism constitutes another of our vicious cycles. The "success" of active terrorists boosts the self-esteem of passive terrorists, giving them a sense of victory and power. In turn, the pride felt by passive terrorists prepares the ground for active terrorists and gives them the tacit approval to continue. Within the Muslim community, passive terrorists often behave quite actively by suppressing truly moderate voices. This suppression typically takes the form of ostracizing the moderate Muslim and his family, or by using harsh language, physical threats, and even violence.[19] Outside of the community, support for terror often takes the form of *taqiyya*, or misleading the "enemy" (with the idea of weakening him). One example of the *taqiyya* employed by Islamists is to provide Westerners different interpretations of Quranic verses from the ones they utilize themselves. For example, many Islamic organizations and scholars attempt to prove to Westerners that Islam promotes freedom of religion, by citing {Quran 2:256}: *Let there be no compulsion in religion.* This sounds excellent, until we realize that many of the same scholars also support *Redda* Law, which enjoins Muslims to kill apostates or kill any Muslim who denies a fundamental component of Islam. Note that it is inadequate to simply proclaim the "freedom to leave Islam", as some fake moderates do, because such moderates still permit Muslims to kill those individuals who have "freely" left the faith. These expressions of "moderation" are deceiving to

---

[19]*See, for example: "Inside Islam: Faith vs. Fanatics" from the documentary series "Islam versus Islamists", aired on FoxNews, October 20, 2007, http://www.foxnews.com/story/0,2933,303381,00.html; This episode was scheduled to be aired on PBS, but was too politically-incorrect. After negotiations with the producers and PBS, it was aired on Fox. The DVD Series can be purchased online: http://www.islamdocumentary.com/*

Westerners. There is no substitute for rejecting Redda Law in its entirety.

Similarly, many of these scholars proclaim to Westerners that Islam does not force a non-Muslim to convert. But there is an unspoken qualification: Salafi teaching grants a non-Muslim the right to practice his faith, but only as a *dhimmi* who agrees to pay the *jizya*. In the view of these Islamic bodies, this is tolerance and mercy. Non-Muslims are perfectly free not to convert – as long as they agree to live as second-class citizens and pay a demeaning poll-tax. These justifications for Islam as a Religion of Peace can only be meaningful if the same Islamic scholars denounced the barbaric Redda Law and insisted that non-Muslims be treated as equals, not as dhimmi.

Alarm at the widespread, passive support for Islamic terror is not unwarranted – there is hard data. In the Arab world, a recent poll on Al-Jazeera Arabic TV (figure 2) showed that 57.9% of viewers support the views of Ayman Al-Zawahiri, as he expressed them in a videotape.

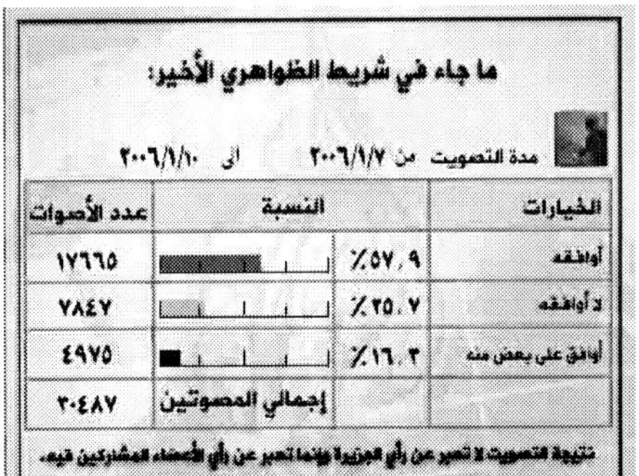

ما جاء في شريط الظواهري الأخير:

مدة التصويت من ٢٠٠٦/١/٧ الى ٢٠٠٦/١/١٠

الخيارات	النسبة		عدد الأصوات
أوافقه	٪٥٧,٩		١٧٦٦٥
لا أوافقه	٪٢٥,٧		٧٨٤٧
أوافق على بعض منه	٪١٦,٣		٤٩٧٥
		إجمالي المصوتين	٣٠٤٨٧

نتيجة التصويت لا تعبر عن رأي الجزيرة وإنما تعبر عن رأي الأعضاء المشتركين فيه.

Figure 2: Al Jazeera Poll, taken July 1, 2006 – October 1, 2006, which shows support for Al-Zawahiri's views.

Al-Jazeera conducted a similar poll between the 12th and 15th of April, 2004. Viewers were asked whether they supported the kidnapping and killing of innocent civilians in Iraq. More than 75% responded in the affirmative:

عدد الأصوات	النسبة		الخيارات
	مدة التصويت: من2004/04/19 إلى 2004/04/26		
	موضوع التصويت:		
	هل تعتقد أن استهداف العاملين في شركات أجنبية لطردها من العراق أمر مجد؟		
1931		75.5%	نعم
625		24.5%	لا
2556	إجمالي التصويتين		
	نتيجة التصويت لا تعبر عن رأي الجزيرة وإنما تعبر عن رأي الأعضاء المشاركين فيه.		

Similarly, Al-Jazeera conducted a poll to see the percentage of the Arab viewers who would support Al Qaeda attacks in Algeria against innocent civilians. More than 50% of 30,000 responding viewers supported these attacks:

عدد الأصوات	النسبة		الخيارات
	مدة التصويت: من2007/12/12 إلى 2007/12/15		
	موضوع التصويت:		
	هل تؤيد هجمات القاعدة في الجزائر؟		
16400		54.7%	نعم
13609		45.3%	لا
30009	إجمالي التصويتين		
	نتيجة التصويت لا تعبر عن رأي الجزيرة وإنما تعبر عن رأي الأعضاء المشاركين فيه.		

The situation is little better in the UK. According to polls, between 40% and 60% of British Muslims would prefer to live under Sharia law; nearly 25% said the 7/7 bombings in London were justified by Britain's participation in the war on terror; and nearly half think 9/11 was a conspiracy between the US and Israel.[20]

---

[20] Melanie Philips, "Do not appease hatred", *The Australian*, March 2, 2007, http://www.theaustralian.news.com.au/story/0,20867,21309355-7583,00. html

Similar conclusions can be drawn from results of recent Pew Global Attitudes Surveys, which polled Muslims in America and abroad. The authors of one Pew study did their best to characterize the results as positive, but despite their efforts, the results are discouraging. 8% of American Muslims believe that suicide bombing is sometimes justified and the results are worse for Muslims between the ages of 19 and 35. Among the younger crowd, 15% believe suicide bombing is sometimes justified. Conservatively estimated, there are 2.3 million Muslims in the US, so we have 184,000 American Muslims who believe that suicide bombing is sometimes justified. Furthermore, these numbers do not show the percentage of Muslims who accept terrorist acts by techniques other than suicide bombings. Also, a significant percentage of respondents are likely to have answered dishonestly, since it is in the interest of Islamists to deceive their host nations about their true intentions. As we can see, the numbers are far from heartening when we examine them carefully. The more Islamists seem moderate in poll results, the more host nations are lulled into complacency.

Passive Denial

The recent Pew survey also shows that 60% of American Muslims do not believe that Arabs perpetrated the 9/11 attacks – a result made more bizarre because bin Laden himself stated in one of his authentic videotapes that he was responsible. This denial, a form of passive terrorism, occurs for a number of reasons.

For one, it presents Islamists with a conundrum. If they admitted that Bin Laden was behind September 11, they would either have to support him or denounce him. If they supported him it would reveal their hand to Western host countries prematurely. If they denounced him, they would betray their Muslim brother. To avoid this "Catch 22", many Muslims skirt the issue by claiming that bin Laden, and Arabs in general, were not behind the attacks. Of course, somebody or some organization must have been responsible, so other perpetrators are suggested. Efforts have been made by Muslims to convince the world that a conspiratorial cabal of Jews was behind it, or that it was an "inside job" by US intelligence agencies. This redirection of blame serves a secondary purpose of refocusing anger toward Americans and Jews.

True enough, a percentage of respondents probably deny bin Laden's involvement out of shame; although it is not clear how sizable this number is. Arab culture places a high priority on Honor. It has been characterized, in fact, as a "shame based" culture. Muslims worry about their image, not realizing that denial only harms it further. *Redemption from shame is not and cannot ever be the product of denial.* It comes, rather from honestly admitting defects and then confronting them openly, specifically, and vigorously.

It is true, therefore, that fear plays a role in passivity – it prevents peaceful Muslims from taking charge of their communities. However, the numbers of Moderate Muslims should not be overstated – one can see why by reasoning about poll results. If it were true that Muslims deny or passively support Islamic terror out of fear, then one imagines that an anonymous poll would be their best opportunity to express their disagreement and dissatisfaction. There is no risk in doing so – the community will not know who answered and will not be able to target dissenters. Yet the polls show a disappointing degree of support and denial, hardly the number of moderates that we would hope for.

False Uproar, Deafening Silence

Recent events show that the Muslim community across the globe is prepared to protest in large numbers, loudly and angrily. It is not a disorganized, apathetic community. But what have they protested? We have seen violent demonstrations against Pope Benedict XVI because he cited a historical text critical of Islam. We have seen cities everywhere erupt in mayhem because a Danish newspaper published a cartoon of Muhammad which depicted him with a bomb on his head. France banned the wearing of the *hijab* in public schools, and Muslims took to the streets.

Equally meaningful, is what the Muslim community has not protested. Unfortunately, we have seen not one protest explicitly against Osama bin Laden and other specific terrorists and terrorist organizations. Nor have we seen any appreciable protest to the incessant and massive violence between Muslims. Take the case of the Bangladeshi War of Independence from Pakistan. During this civil war, Bangladesh estimates it lost upward of 3 million in what is almost certainly genocide. Mass graves are still being uncovered today. Although outside estimates of the death toll are lower (Pakistan estimates 26,000, the UN between 200,000 and 3 million), there is no question that the toll was profoundly large. However, beyond the mass-murder, it is noteworthy that both sides were Sunni Muslim. At the time, Pakistani Muslim scholars issued a *fatwa* enjoining the forces to rape any Bangladeshi women captured, citing the Quran and claiming any incident of rape to be justified by the religion (*Ma-Malkakat Aymanikum*). It is estimated that more than 20,000 women were raped.[21]

Where was the outrage of the global Muslim community? So silent was it, that today even educated Westerners are unlikely to be familiar with the war and its atrocities.

Protest for the world's Muslims typically takes two forms: public demonstration and statements, and the *fatwa*. A *fatwa*

---

[21]For example: "1971 Bangladesh Pakistan War Criminals", http://ghatok-dalal.tripod.com/
The Wikipedia entry fails to mention the *fatwa* and shamefully understates the Islamic component in the war:
Wikipedia contributors, "Bangladesh Liberation War," *Wikipedia, The Free Encyclopedia*, http://en.wikipedia.org/w/index.php?title=Bangladesh_Liberation_War&oldid=178924681 (accessed December 21, 2007)

is simply a judicial decree by an Islamic religious body. The plural form, in Arabic, is *fatawa*, and there are *fatawa* for nearly everything: marital relations, table manners, rules of war, how to properly have sex, and so on. The *fatwa* is also used for purposes relevant to our topic. It is used to declare a person an apostate (similar to excommunication, but with dire consequences). It can declare an act to be un-Islamic, and it may define who is a Muslim and who is not.

After 9/11, we have, actually, seen a few Muslim demonstrations and *fatawa* against "Terrorism". But this terrorism could be anything violent whatsoever. One often hears that an Israeli reprisal against Palestinian attacks is "Terrorism", or that American military involvement in the Middle East is "Terrorism". The word is deliberately left vague. It has no agent; who is the perpetrator? Whom should we bring to justice? The word is easily manipulated by those who wish to deceive Western citizens.

In Arab culture, denouncing a crime is not taken seriously unless one denounces the criminal by name. Failure to ascribe responsibility for a criminal act is understood by the perpetrator to be not only a tacit approval of his deed, but a cover for it. This applies to passive terrorism – denouncing "Terrorism" without explicitly denouncing an agent is both an endorsement and a cover.

So while we have seen a few demonstrations and *fatawa* against "Terrorism", we have seen a dearth of condemnation by Muslims of specific Islamic *terrorists and groups*. When we are able to observe masses of Muslims demonstrating against bin Laden and al-Qaeda, then we can claim definitively that the majority of Muslims are against him. Without seeing this explicit admonishment, claiming that most Muslims oppose Islamic terrorists is dubious speculation. This requirement of specificity should embrace another requirement: that Muslims denounce terrorists for the right reason. One example of a bad and dangerous motivation is to denounce terrorism because it "damages the image of Islam" or that it sometimes kills Muslims (would it be fine if it only killed non-Muslims?). Terrorists read these admonishments as they are intended: violence is acceptable as long as it doesn't damage Islam's image, and that it is acceptable as long as targets are restricted to non-Muslims.

This ambiguous denouncement of Islamic terror is a recurring and significant problem. Such denouncements, when they happen, do not denounce the general war against non-Islamic civilization and do not denounce terrorism simply because it is immoral and barbaric. The vast majority of statements issued by Islamic organizations have avoided denouncing Osama bin Laden by name; at best they denounce "those who perpetrated the attack", which is deliberately ambiguous and problematic. On the rare occasion when bin Laden is mentioned, it is to express regret that he also murdered Muslims in the Trade Centers.

When Saudi Religious authorities denounce the terrorists, they typically use the phrase, *Al-Fiaa Al-Dala*, or "those who are on the wrong path" (perhaps also, "the misguided"). This condemnation has since become ubiquitous and is understood in Arabic to be extremely mild, as one might expect from the translation. It is taken for granted that *Al-Fiaa Al-Dala* are not apostates, but mistaken believers. The phrase is popular because it seems to satisfy Westerners in the "export market" while dulling the blade of rebuke at home. Another phrase used for "terrorist" is *irhabi*, plural, *irhabeen*. Sheikh Abdel Rahman took this label as a badge of honor, after the 1993 Trade Center attack, by citing a Quranic verse:

Against them (The Infidels) make ready your strength to the utmost of your power, including steeds of war, to strike terror into (the hearts of) the enemies, of Allah and your enemies, and others besides, whom ye may not know, but whom Allah doth know. Whatever ye shall spend in the cause of Allah, shall be repaid unto you, and ye shall not be treated unjustly.
{Quran 8:60}

Islamic jargon does have very powerful words to denounce the terrorists. The strongest possible condemnation can be expressed by calling terrorists *Al-Murtadeen*, literally, "the apostates". This is not simply a tactical invention; there is precedent for it. It was originally used by the first Caliph, Abu Bakr, to designate those who failed to pay the Islamic charity tithe, or *zaka*. A war was fought against this group, known as the *Redda* War, from which we get *Redda* Law, or the law concerning apostates. The phrase *Al-Murtadeen* is extremely strong, and unfortunately, it is rarely if ever used to refer to terrorists. It isn't perfect, of course; it suggests that anyone who commits terror isn't Muslim, an assertion that yields different (but preferable) complications. It also implies that the named terrorist should be killed (a good thing) because he is an apostate (a bad reason). Still, it is the strongest condemnation available in Islamic jurisprudence and will help make Jihadism more unsavory to young Muslims. Certainly, it is preferable to the phrase used the day after 9/11 by the Saudi sheikh, Salman Al-Uda, to describe Osama bin Laden: "my brother".[22] The sheikh helpfully added that bin Laden's actions have a negative impact on Islam, from which we can infer that his actions would be fine if they didn't have a negative impact on Islam's reputation.

Public statements and *fatawa* sometimes masquerade as peaceful and "moderate", but under careful scrutiny, also exhibit ambiguity and deliberate leeway for interpreting it as approval. These *fatawa* placate Westerners who take the peaceful tone at face value, but they do not deter young Muslims from jihad. Over the years, I have assembled a not-insubstantial collection of terrorism-related statements and *fatawa*; for the sake of brevity, let us contrast a small sampling

---

[22]Scott MacLeod, comment on "News Flash: Muslim Denounces Terrorism!", *Time Magazine Blogs: The Middle East*, comment posted September 22, 2007, http://time-blog.com/middle_east/2007/09/news_flash_muslim_denounces_te.html

of them to the *fatwa* issued against Salman Rushdie for his publication of the bestselling *Satanic Verses*. The contrast is remarkable and highlights the insidious nature of the dual-purpose *fatwa*.

Strong condemnation, Rushdie:

> *In the name of God Almighty. There is only one God, to whom we shall all return. I would like to inform all intrepid Muslims in the world that the author of the book entitled The Satanic Verses, which has been compiled, printed, and published in opposition to Islam, the Prophet, and the Qur'an, as well as those publishers who were aware of its contents, have been sentenced to death. I call on all zealous Muslims to execute them quickly, wherever they find them, so that no one will dare insult the Islamic sanctities. Whoever is killed on this path will be regarded as a martyr, God willing. In addition, anyone who has access to the author of the book, but does not possess the power to execute him, should refer him to the people so that he may be punished for his actions. May God's blessing be on you all.*
> Ruhollah Musavi Khomeini [Grand Ayatollah, Supreme Leader, Iran]

Compare:

> *[T]he September 11 terrorist blasts in America can only be the job of a group that have voluntarily severed their own ears and tongues, so that the only language with which they could communicate would be destroying and spreading death.*
> Muhammad Khatami [President of Iran]

This looks like an impressive condemnation, until we realize that Khatami never says the attacks of 9/11 were actually wrong. He simply stated that the terrorists – whoever they are – didn't have any other means of expressing themselves.

In America, condemnations seem much better but are also highly flawed:

> *WASHINGTON, DC – The American-Arab Anti-Discrimination Committee (ADC) today condemned the horrifying series of attacks on the World Trade Center towers in New York and government buildings including the Pentagon in Washington DC. Arab Americans, like all Americans, are shocked and angered by such*

brutality, and we share all the emotions of our fellow citizens. Arab Americans view these attacks as targeting all Americans without exception. … No information is available as to what individuals or organizations might be responsible for these attacks. No matter who is responsible, ADC condemns these actions in the strongest possible terms. ADC urges the public and the media to proceed with caution and to resist rushes to judgment.[23]

This *fatwa* not only fails to mention Osama bin Laden and condemn him in the strongest possible terms, it actually asserts that we do not even know who committed the atrocity. Furthermore, instead of keeping attention on the 3000 murdered, it quickly launches into defense of Arab Americans while the victim's bodies are still warm, which seems unnecessary if it isn't clear who the perpetrators were. Most importantly, 9/11 attacks did more than target Americans – they targeted freedom and decency around the world – all nations.

Here is a *fatwa* issued by CAIR, the Council of American Islamic relations, immediately subsequent to 9/11:

We at the Council on American Islamic Relations (CAIR), along with the entire American Muslim community are deeply saddened by the massive loss of life resulting from the tragic events of September 11. American Muslims utterly condemn the vicious and cowardly acts of terrorism against innocent civilians. We join with all Americans in calling for the swift apprehension and punishment of the perpetrators. No political cause could ever be assisted by such immoral acts.

In this *fatwa*, what are we to make of the phrase "political cause"? What about religious causes? And are Israelis or Thai Buddhists "innocent"? Is it fine to use terrorism against those considered "guilty" by the Islamic establishment? Rest assured, jihadists know how to interpret this *fatwa*.

---

[23]"ADC Condemns Attack on Trade Center, Government Buildings", *American-Arab Anti-Discrimination Committee*, September 11, 2001, http://www.adc.org/index.php?id=1252&no_cache=1&sword_list%5b%5d=world&sword_list%5b%5d=trade&sword_list%5b%5d=center

Elsewhere, we find weighing-in (about 9/11) a certain Sheikh Rached Ghannouchi, chairman of Tunisia's an-Nahda Movement, currently in exile in England:

> *Such destruction can only be condemned by any Muslim, however resentful one may be of America's biased policies supporting occupation in Palestine, as an unacceptable attack on thousands of innocent people having no relation to American policies. Anyone familiar with Islam has no doubt about its rejection of collective punishment, based on the well-known Quranic principle that 'no bearer of burdens can bear the burden of another.*[24]

We have already shown that the Israeli/Palestinian conflict is not the reason for global terror, that it is used by Islamists as a diversion. Jihadists will take this *fatwa* to mean that their rage is understandable, and the lack of direct attribution to bin Laden will also be read as a go-ahead. Critical here is the phrase "innocent people having no relation to American policies". Is this to mean that terrorism is justified against those connected with US policy? As one might expect, the answer is "Yes". In fact, jihadists view every American as being responsible for American policies because Americans elect their government.

The calculated dissembling of Yusuf al-Qaradawi furnishes us with another instructive example. Qaradawi is a famous and highly regarded Islamic scholar born in Egypt (now residing in Qatar). Qaradawi is regarded as a moderate by many in the West, for example, by Ken Livingston (mayor of London), or Raymond William Baker (historian), who hails Qaradawi as a democratic reformer. Here are Qaradawi's thoughts about the September 11 attacks:

> *We Arab Muslims are the most affected by the grave consequences of hostile attack on man and life. We share the suffering experienced by innocent Palestinians at the hands of the tyrannical Jewish entity who raze the Palestinian homes to the ground, set fire to their tilth, kill them cold-bloodedly, and leave innocent orphans wailing behind….*

---

[24]The Washington Post, October 13, 2001, p. B9; citation found online at http://www.unc.edu/~kurzman/terror.htm

With this in mind, the daily life in Palestine has become a permanent memorial gathering. When Palestinians face such unjust aggression, they tend to stem bloodletting and destruction and not to claim the lives of innocent civilians…. I categorically go against a committed Muslim's embarking on such attacks. Islam never allows a Muslim to kill the innocent and the helpless…. If such attacks were carried out by a Muslim - as some biased groups claim - then we, in the name of our religion, deny the act and incriminate the perpetrator. We do confirm that the aggressor deserves the deterrent punishment irrespective of his religion, race or gender…. What we warn against, even if it becomes a reality, is to hold a whole nation accountable for a crime carried out by a limited number of people or to characterize a certain religion as a faith giving support to violence and terrorism.[25]

Qaradawi doesn't seem to know who perpetrated 9/11, but whoever did, they certainly are frustrated by the plight of the Palestinians at the hands of Israelis. It helps to be familiar with Qaradawi's other public statements. He believes, for example, that all Israelis are guilty and are therefore legitimate targets. In other words, blowing up an Israeli school bus is fine because no Israeli is innocent. He can't seem to muster very strong criticism for bin Laden, either. In an interview with French Scholar Gilles Kepel, Qaradawi was asked for his opinion of bin Laden:

[bin Laden] has never published anything that would allow one to judge his learning on actual evidence; he could not possibly call himself a doctor in law, and therefore can pass no juridical opinion, or fatwa: he is a 'preacher'—the lowest rank in the current hierarchical classification.

The problem with bin Laden, thinks Qaradawi, is not that he is a brutal mass-murderer, but that he is a lousy scholar.[26]

There are countless examples of such statements and *fatawa*, but we will examine one more – a *fatwa* that shows

---

[25]"Sheikh Yusuf Al-Qaradawi Condemns Attacks Against Civilians: Forbidden in Islam", *IslamOnline*, September 13, 2001, http://www.islamonline. net/English/News/2001-09/13/article25.shtml

[26]See the excellent piece by Lee Smith, "The Myth of Islamist Democracy", *Slate*, July 16, 2004 http://www.slate.com/id/2103980/

how incredibly subtle the dual nature can be. This *fatwa* to condemn terrorism was issued by the "Amman Conference", a collaboration of the most renowned international Islamic bodies, representing all the major *madhab*, or schools of jurisprudence. The full text can be found in the Appendix, but here we will examine one highlight:

> [I]t is not possible to declare whosoever subscribes to the Ash'ari creed or whoever practices true Sufism an apostate. Likewise, it is not possible to declare whosoever subscribes to true Salafi thought an apostate. Equally, it is not possible to declare as apostates any group of Muslims who believes in Allah the Mighty and Sublime and His Messenger (may Peace and Blessings be upon him) and the pillars of faith, and respects the pillars of Islam and does not deny any "Maloom Mina Al-Din Bil-Darura" - necessary article of religion.

Here, what is meant by "true Sufism" or "true Salafi"? jihadists know they can always claim their targets aren't "true" Sufists or Salafists, and therefore, killing could be justified. How is one to empirically determine if a professed Muslim actually "believes in Allah the Mighty" or is merely putting on a show? Similarly, what is meant by "necessary article of religion"? Here too, jihadists can claim that their targets didn't follow necessary articles. All of these flaws, however, pale in comparison with two overarching defects: the *fatwa* does not condemn the killing of apostates and it does not condemn the killing of non-Muslims – it merely attempts (and fails) to narrow the criteria for apostasy.

As we can see, passive terrorism is a widespread, pernicious problem. Large swaths of the Muslim community quietly ignore Islamism or secretly approve of it. While Muslims protest every perceived insult to Islam by the West with loud, widespread demonstrations that are often violent and always intimidating, they do not similarly demonstrate against the "hijiacking" of their religion. Islamic terror is not likely to decrease until Muslims cease being passive terrorists and start becoming active defenders of hard truth, true peace, and real tolerance.

Theological Deception

One of the tactics that Islamists use to deceive the West is to present the same religious information to non-Muslims in one way and to Muslims in another. For example, it was common after September 11th to find Islamic scholars using the following hadith to convince Westerners that jihad means "peaceful struggle":

> *You have come from the minor jihad to the major jihad."...then he said "it is the striving of the servant against his desires."*

Certainly, this hadith could yield a peaceful understanding of the word "jihad", but unfortunately, distinguished Islamic books teach that it is a *weak* Hadith. For example, Abu Bakr Al-Jazairy – a lecturer in the Nobel Prophetic Mosque in Saudi Arabia – wrote in his well-known, widely-distributed book, Minhaj Al-Muslim, that this hadith

> *...is based upon a weak Hadith that was reported by Al-Baihaqi and Al-Khateeb in the Tarikh. They reported it from Jabir.*
> Minhaj Al-Muslim, Volume 2, Page 167

As we can see, on the one hand Islamists show non-Muslims a peaceful hadith to improve Islam's image, and on the other teach Muslims, that it is weak (and by implication, that Muslims should not follow it).

In contrast, Islamists teach Muslims that the following hadith is *sahih*, or "strong", "accurate" and "authentic", and thus cannot be ignored:

> *I have been commanded to fight all mankind until they testify that none has the right to be worshiped except Allah and Muhammad is the messenger of Allah, they perform the Salah (the five prayers) and pay the Zakah (obligatory Charity). If they do this, they have protected their blood and their wealth from me except by the right of Islam and their reckoning will be with Allah the almighty. (Agreed upon)*
> Minhaj Al-Muslim, Volume 1, Page 402

The phrase "agreed upon" at the end of the above hadith means that it is narrated as *sahih* by both *Al-Buchary* and

Muslim, which communicates to Muslims that it is extremely powerful. Using such hadiths as justification, some disciples of Prophet Muhammad declared wars on non-Muslims to subjugate them to Islam. In this case, Muslims are taught that the violent hadith is strong and the peaceful hadith is weak. This theological tactic deceives countless non-Muslims.

Another example of this theological deception is the hadith used by many Muslims to make Islamic teaching look peaceful:

> *Whoever harms a non-Muslim citizen (of the Islamic state), then I will be his opponent on the day of resurrection.*

This is certainly a fantastic hadith, but in Minhaj we find:

> *Recorded by Al-Khateeb and it is weak.*
> Minhaj Al-Muslim, Volume 1, Page 226

Here again, the peaceful hadith is the weak one, and once again, the same world-renowned Islamic book teaches that the following hadith is strong:

> *Do not initiate the greetings of peace with the Jews and the Christians. If you meet any one of them on the road, force him to go to the narrowest part of it." (Muslim)*

As before, the appended word *Muslim* at the end of this hadith refers to the fact that it is written in *Sahih Muslim*, which is considered by most Muslims as one of the two most authentic Islamic books for *sahih* ("accurate") hadiths. It bears repeating that the author of *Minhaj* is merely referencing mainstream Islamic teaching. He is not the one who classified the hadiths; the accuracy of the hadith is not his opinion.

In short, what is being told to Westerners is not what is being taught to young Muslims. Many Westerners incorrectly conclude that Islam is a "Religion of Peace" based on these peaceful hadiths. Unfortunately, Islamists teach that these peaceful hadiths are weak, that they should be ignored, and that the violent Hadith are *sahih* ("authentic").

Shifting the Blame

When some Muslims react to criticism directed at their community, perceptive observers often note that this reaction is almost always defensive, and sometimes hostile. Similarly, when Muslims are confronted with questions about terror, they point the finger at America, or Israel, or a conspiracy – anything but themselves. This refusal to take personal responsibility for their actions is a gigantic stumbling block to preventing terror and treating the Islamist disease in the community at large. It is also a problem that one sees to a much lesser extent among other groups. In America, thousands protested their own government's policies over Vietnam, civil rights, free speech, abortion, and more. In Israel, thousands of Jews protested their country's involvement in Lebanon during the 1980s. Yet we rarely see Muslims take members of their own community "to the woodshed".

By now, it may not surprise the reader to learn that this lack of personal responsibility has roots in Salafi Islam. In Arab societies, it is not uncommon to hear the phrase: *Al shaitan wa zenne* – "Satan has inspired me", or as it is said in English, "The devil made me do it". Every year during the *haj*, pilgrims circle a symbol of Satan and throw rocks at it with great vehemence. The purpose is to express anger at Satan for making them sin and to deter him from doing so in the future. They are not responsible for their sinning, the devil is. Young Muslim children are taught and often forced to memorize the following *sura*:

> I ask refuge with the God of all humans …the king of all humans…
> From the mischief of the Whisperer (of Evil), who withdraws (after his whisper)
> {Quran: 114:1-4}

In this verse, it is widely understood that the "Whisperer" is Satan, or *Shaitan*. The verse rhymes in Arabic, making it particularly easy to remember.

The consistent attribution of mistakes to the devil creates a mentality where each individual does not consider himself responsible for any problem. Once the Muslim learns to blame the devil, it is easy to characterize any external force as either the devil or his work. Thus, America is the "Great Satan", responsible for most problems in the Muslim world. This culture of deflection makes it very difficult for the Muslim community to correct itself, because it will not acknowledge its responsibility for the crisis in the first place.

Who is a "Moderate Muslim"?

Many non-Muslim Westerners will tell you that the majority of Muslims are "moderates". It is a persistent theme in public discourse and has become an obligatory preface to discussing Islamism. In itself, this fact should be disconcerting – it doesn't seem to be necessary to speak of "moderate Buddhists", and we rarely hear exhortations to "moderate Christianity". Intrinsic to the phrase "moderate Islam" is the problematic implication of its necessity. Apparently, most people suspect there is some sort of problem associated with Islam – they merely fear articulating what that problem is or admitting its extent. It is a rare person who offers a precise definition of "moderate" as it pertains to Muslims; we almost never hear a clear delineation of criteria which can be used to identify one. Similarly, we should be prepared to accept whatever determination is made about the Muslim population that results from our inquiries, and not attempt to "reverse engineer" the facts to fit comfortable preconceptions. In short, any Muslim could be a moderate when we lack a clear understanding of what the word signifies.

When those who use the phrase "moderate" are pressed as to what they mean, they sometimes define a moderate Muslim as one who does not commit a terrorist act. Unfortunately, this makes most suicide bombers moderates until the very minute of the explosion. In fact, many of the Islamic terrorists we have seen in Europe recently (London, Madrid) were considered very moderate prior to revelation of their involvement. Before 9/11, the hijackers looked in every way assimilated – many were clean-shaven, wore jeans and t-shirts, and would even visit strip clubs. Neighbors of the 9/11 hijackers were shocked when superficially irreligious acquaintances were found to be violent agents of fundamentalist Islam.

How is this possible? One tactic of jihadists is to deceive the infidel until he is weakened and thereby ripe for conquest. It actually has a word: *taqiyya*. Jihadists who assimilate into infidel societies in order to wage jihad are not considered un-Islamic. Zawahiri himself advocated this approach. Unfortunately, this form of *taqiyya* applies not only to active terrorists preparing an attack, but to passive terrorists. Superficial indications of secularism, modernity, hospitality, and westernization simply cannot be used as a guide to determine who is moderate.

Indeed, Muslims who in every respect are kind and gracious can harbor Salafist religious beliefs and hatred for non-Islamic societies. In cases where it is unconscious, it can be termed "Double Mind Theory" (DMT), a psychological condition similar to George Orwell's notion of "Double Think". We have seen "Double Think" most notably among Soviet citizens, who described their own society in their criticisms of the West. DMT is part of a larger psychological paradigm known as *cognitive dissonance* – the capacity to believe in mutually contradictory notions without being aware of it. In the case of passive terrorists, the schism is one between the cultural mind and the religious mind.

It is an integral part of Arab culture to show great hospitality to guests, and Muslim Middle Easterners in Western societies often show such hospitality to their neighbors. Depressingly often, however, their religious mind could at the same time support declaring war on Infidels to subjugate them to Islam. This contradiction has lead to confusion among many Westerners. An instructive example is that of Jim Carrol, a peace activist taken hostage in Iraq in 2006. She was released after three months of captivity and promptly spoke to the media, where she enthused about her kidnappers' hospitality. These same kidnappers were planning terrorist attacks and indicated so to her.

Whichever mind is dominant at a given time determines hospitality or aggression. The presence of a religious mind that accepts violent religious teachings is the primary reason that most Muslims do not demonstrate with any real zeal against bin Laden, or why the highest Islamic organizations cannot bring themselves to issue a *fatwa* of apostasy against him.

A natural definition of moderate might be "non-Salafist", but then objections are raised that some are "mild" Salafists. Perhaps it is possible to distinguish between "hard-core" Salafists and "mild" Salafists; but whenever a Muslim promotes the view that Sharia should be the single binding law, with all its violent edicts and oppressive rules, or seeks to emulate ancient codes of dress and behavior, that Muslim, whether he denies it or not, is a Salafist. After 9/11, I have actually met Salafi Muslims who claim to Westerners that they are Sufi with the goal of appearing moderate. Many wonder why there has been so little outcry or protest by the Islamic mainstream against promotion of Sharia. The answer is that much of the Islamic mainstream is Salafist and actually supports Sharia.

While it is very difficult to find mainstream clerics and mainstream Islamic books that stand unambiguously against Salafi tenets, it is easy to find examples of militancy and obfuscation. According to Omar M. Ahmad, Chairmain of the Board on the Council of American Islamic Relations:

> *Islam isn't in America to be equal to any other faith but to become dominant. The Koran, the Muslim book of scripture, should be the highest authority in America, and Islam the only accepted religion on Earth.*

Omar denies having said this, despite witnesses to the contrary, and has worked up a good dose of outrage. CAIR is considered to be a preeminent mainstream Islamic organization in the US. In fact, the organization's mission statement proclaims, "CAIR's mission is to enhance understanding of Islam, encourage dialogue, protect civil liberties, empower American Muslims, and build coalitions that promote justice and mutual understanding."[27] Yet according to columnist Joseph Farah, "You should see the hate mail I get from CAIR's members. It would make your hair stand on end."[28] When asked about the overwhelming numbers of Muslims in the terrorist ranks, CAIR executive director Nihad Awad, obfuscates:

> They are Muslim, but they're not Islamic. Their actions are not inspired by Islam. It's like Islam philosophy.[29]

In other words, terrorism isn't fueled by Salafism and terrorists aren't Salafists – it is the product of un-Islamic Muslim Islamic Philosophers. CAIR's Florida Communications Director, Ahmed Bedier, is no better. He informed Florida Representative Ginny Browne-Waite:

> Catholic priests pose more of a terrorism threat by having sex with young altar boys than those who flew planes into the World Trade Center.[30]

In 2006 I attended the Secular Islam Summit – a conference to which CAIR objected strenuously. CNN's Glen Beck was on-

---

[27]"Our Vision, Mission, and Core Principles", Council on American Islamic-Relations, http://www.cair.com/AboutUs/VisionMissionCorePrinciples.aspx (accessed December 21, 2007)

[28]Art Moore, "Should Muslim Quran be USA's top authority?", World-NetDaily, May 1, 2003, http://www.worldnetdaily.com/news/article.asp?ARTICLE_ID=32341

[29]"CAIR Outraged Over President's Use of Term 'Islamic Fascists'", FoxNews Online, August 15, 2006, http://www.foxnews.com/story/0,2933,208433,00.html

[30]Daniel Pipes, comment on "CAIR Criticized", Daniel Pipes' Weblog, comment posted July 16, 2003, http://www.danielpipes.org/blog/38

site to cover it and he wanted to get perspectives from both sides, so he interviewed Bedier and me on his show. Bedier objected that I wasn't American, that I didn't understand Islam in America, and that I couldn't genuinely represent American Muslims. He added, "In order to have legitimate reform, you need to have the right messengers". Bedier was speaking as if Islam is taught in America from different resources than Islam that is taught in other parts of the world. A single visit to any Islamic book store in the US will reveal that violence and intolerance are taught here as they are being taught in Islamic countries. The same Salafi references are used and recommended in both places. In addition, September 11 was orchestrated outside American borders. Looking at the threat of Islamism only within the borders of the US – as Mr. Bedier did – is therefore a very primitive and shallow approach to the problem.

Salafism permeates a wide variety of Islamic organizations that rarely call themselves Salafist. However, merely by accepting or not clearly opposing the violent laws of Sharia they reveal themselves to be in the Salafi camp. Although Salafists fear, hate, and fight against modern values of freedom and civil rights, Salafists nevertheless complain bitterly about violations of their civil rights when they reside in modern societies. Such complaints, however, are tactical – the goal is to establish a Sharia-based society with no civil rights, by achieving strength in non-Sharia societies. Just as Salafists seek to "use democracy to end democracy", as they have done in Algeria, for example, so to do they employ the civil protections of modern nations with the goal of ending civil protections. Civil protections, in the Salafi mind, are weaknesses that can be exploited and even championed for the sake of ultimate Islamic subjugation. It is like parasitic forms of cancer that use the blood and nutrition of the host to grow bigger and destroy that host at the end.

Indeed, Salafists may support a government that implements most aspects of Sharia. Such is the case with Saudi Arabia, where the ruling system was and still is supported by

Wahabbi clerics. Other Salafists, such as Bin Laden, consider Saudi Arabia insufficiently Islamic; the country grants entry to non-Muslims, permits women to be educated and to work in some fields, permits secular TV channels, and justifies the existence of a Western (non-Sharia) banking system.

More common than incitement to violence is the continuous, low-level promulgation and reinforcement of doctrinal justifications for violence and the incitement to commit such acts. A Salafist will normally assert, among fellow adherents, that war should be declared on the infidels when the members gain sufficient strength. Since traditional Islamic teaching agrees on numerous violent or inhumane concepts, it is essential that a Muslim or Islamic scholar stand clearly and unambiguously against them in order to be considered truly peaceful. One way to confront Islamic leaders about Salafism is to ask them pointed questions; to assist in the task, I have developed a practical quiz which we can call the Radical Islam Support Test (RIST).

Apostates:	*Do you support killing them? Should leaving the faith of Islam be punishable by death?*
Beating women:	*Is beating women ever acceptable and if not, do you reject those decrees of Islamic law that sanction the beating of women? Do you also accept stoning women to death for committing adultery?*
Calling Jews "pigs and monkeys":	*Do you believe that Jews are in anyway sub-human and if not, do you reject Quranic interpretations that claim they are?*
Declaring Holy War:	*Do you support declaring war against non-Muslims to subjugate them to Islam? Do you believe that it is fair and reasonable to offer non-Muslims three options: Conversion, Paying the Jizya, or Death?*

Enslavement:	*Do you support the enslavement of female war prisoners and having sex with them as concubines? If not, do you reject those interpretations in Islamic Law, for "Ma-Malkakat Aymanikum", which justifies such actions?*
Fighting Jews:	*Do you support perpetual war against Jews to exterminate them, and if not, should those Muslims who incite such war be punished?*[31]
Gays being killed:	*Do you believe it is acceptable to kill Gays, and if not, do you reject those edicts in Sharia Law which claim it is?*

One day I was speaking in a public gathering in Michigan. During the speech, an Imam in the audience stood up and proclaimed that he was a moderate. I responded by asking him if he was prepared to invite Jewish representatives to attend Friday prayers at his mosque, and also if he would state clearly before his congregation that Jews are not pigs and monkeys. The Imam looked down, stepped back, and said nothing.

If a Muslim or Islamic organization fails this quiz, they can safely be regarded as Salafists regardless of any title they use to describe themselves. We can speak endlessly of peaceful Muslims when we focus on the cultural mind. However, when we evaluate the religious mind the outcome can be something else entirely. The question is simple and clear: can a Muslim who believes in the violent concepts outlined by RIST by considered a moderate? If a Muslim is truly moderate, he should not hesitate to clearly and unambiguously reject hateful aspects of Sharia.

The central problem which we face is that the violent injunctions of Sharia – a sampling of which can be found

---

[31]Policy makers should note: this clerical promulgation and widespread belief is a major obstacle to solving the Arab/Israeli conflict.

in our test – are not bizarre, extremist or anachronistic Islamic interpretations, but are mainstream tenets. They are promoted in approved Islamic books. A careful analysis of all the current approved Islamic interpretations and schools of Islamic jurisprudence reveals this root problem.

New interpretations of Islamic texts are essential to our security. Accepting the injunctions of Sharia without extensive reinterpretation prepares the ground for jihadists to take the next logical step. Without providing theologically-based alternatives which clearly reject the injustice and brutality of mainstream Sharia, a war between civilizations is inevitable. Muslims who unquestioningly adhere to a violent value system will eventually force it upon their host nation when their numbers reach critical mass.

Our experience in Iraq has shown that jihadist "insurgents" can put the future of a whole nation at risk. We should not allow the same to happen in the Western world; we cannot allow passive terrorism to fester. Political Correctness should not be allowed to stand in the way. Developing techniques – such as RIST – to determine radical or dangerous views, will not only help keep us safe from Islamism, but will permit true moderate Muslims to flourish without fear of persecution.

Oppression of Women

The plight of women in Islamic societies is appalling in its barbarity and massive in scope. It is well-documented. Although progressive women's movements in the West have been almost entirely silent on the matter, there are a small number of human rights activists, such as Phyllis Chesler, Nonie Darwish, Ayan Hirsi Ali, and others who have worked extensively to raise awareness of the problem.[32] It

---

[32]See, for example, the excellent booklet:
Robert Spencer and Phyllis Chesler, *The Violent Oppression of Women in Islam*, http://www.frontpagemag.com/media/4CDF1CEC-779C-4699-A123-A8992F4D9219/5f35012e-a9b7-4553-abac-efed7da6c983.pdf

is estimated, for example, that over 90% of Pakistani wives have been struck, beaten, or abused sexually. In Iran, a girl is legally marriageable when she reaches the age of nine. To divorce a wife, a Muslim man needs only to say "I divorce you" three times, which leaves the woman with no income and the status of outcast. Recently in Saudi Arabia, a woman was gang raped by four men while a fifth videotaped the event on his camera-phone. The woman received ninety lashes of the whip for being alone in a car with a man who was not her husband. When she appealed, her sentence was more than doubled to 200 lashes. Fortunately, King Abdullah pardoned her after much Western pressure. In addition, Gender Apartheid governs the nation; women are forbidden to drive cars, to vote, to walk in public without wearing the *niqab*. In many parts of the Islamic world, girls undergo clitorectomies – an operation in which girls have their clitoris removed. It is believed that doing so makes a woman chaste and docile. Slavery is still legal in parts of Sudan and Mauritania, which gives rise to sexual slavery. Finally, honor killing is well known to be more prevalent in Muslim communities – both in Islamic countries and in Western nations.

Indeed, the oppression of women in the Islamic world is so involved a topic that it is beyond the scope of a general book about Islamism. While it is a human rights concern by itself, the abuse of women in Islamic societies has another consequence that is less talked about – it contributes extensively to Islamic terror and violence.

To Westerners, the most noticeable aspect of many Muslim women is their dress. After a period of relative liberation in the 1950s and 1960s, women in many Islamic societies began to suffer from proliferating Islamism in the 1970s. They started to wear the *hijab* in greater numbers – in some cases by choice, in others, by force.

Many women leaders in the West have chosen to wear the *hijab* when they conduct diplomatic missions to Islamic states. For example, Nancy Pelosi wore the *hijab* when she visited Bashar Assad of Syria; Laura Bush put one on when she visited Gulf nations in 2007. It isn't related to their own party affiliation or ideological camp – women leaders simply wish to show respect when they conduct diplomacy. These leaders operate under the false belief that the *hijab* is a neutral – or merely traditional – fashion statement, not unlike the *sari* worn by women in India. But the *hijab* is not simply a clothing accessory – it has deep Islamic doctrinal connections to slavery and discrimination. Western women who cover themselves unwittingly endorse an inhumane system.

When I was a member of *Jamaa Islamiya*, we used to despise women who did not wear the *hijab*. We believed they were vain, concerned with earthly pleasures and trivialities, that they would burn in hell. This was based on the following hadith:

> *[It was] narrated by Abu Huraira that Prophet Muhammad said: [there are] two types of people in hell………women who are covered and naked at the same time "Kasiat Areat" [does not cover their body completely]… they walk in a sexy manner and men followed them, their heads shows their hair exposed like the camels' humps….these women will never go to paradise or even smell it.*
> – Sahih Muslim

Within Salafi Islam, the *hijab* serves to differentiate between "free" women and slave girls. In this sense it creates a feeling of superiority among the women who wear it (and their men) toward women who do not.

> *O Prophet! Tell thy wives and daughters (Not the concubines), and the believing (Free) women, that they should cast their outer garments over their bodies, that they should be known (as free women) and thus not molested. And Allah is Oft- Forgiving, Most Merciful.*
> {Quran 33:59}

Tafseer Ibn Kathir (one of the most reputable authorities in explaining the Quran) discusses the context (*Asbab al-nuzil*) of this verse. According to it, some people from Medina would look at a Muslim woman, and if they saw a complete veil or cover they recognized that she was free and thus did not sexually harass her. On the other hand, if a woman was without a veil they marked her as a slave girl and "jumped on her to have sex". The verse exists to differentiate between free women and the concubines so that the free Muslim women would not be molested [*Ibn Kathir*]. Most Islamic authorities and scholars affirm this purpose of the *hijab*.[33] The role that the *hijab* plays in promoting or recognizing slavery is further supported by various hadiths:

> *Narrated Anas: The Prophet stayed for three days between Khaibar (place) and Medina, and there he consummated his marriage to Safiyya bint Huyai (after taking her as a prisoner of war). I invited the Muslims to the wedding banquet in which neither meat nor bread was offered. He ordered for leather dining-sheets to be spread, and dates, dried yoghurt and butter were laid on it, and that was the Prophet's wedding banquet. The Muslims wondered, "Is she (Saffiyya) considered as his wife or his slave girl?" Then they said, "If he orders her to veil herself, she will be one of the mothers of the Believers (the wives of prophet Muhammad); but if he does not order her to veil herself, she will be a slave girl. So when the Prophet proceeded from there, he spared her a space behind him (on his she-camel) and put a screening veil between her and the people (accordingly they understood she became his wife not just his slave girl).*
> – Sahih Al-Buchary

Umar Ibn al-Khattab was one of the foremost disciples of Muhammad. The Prophet personally promised al-Khattab a place in Paradise, so the disciple is a role model for many Muslim men. The behavior of Umar is narrated in many Salafi books, such as those written by *Ibn Tameia*:

> *Umar Ibn Al-khatab used to beat any slave girl if she dared to cover her body as the free Muslim women did; so that free Muslim women become distinctive from the slave girls.*
> Ibn Taimeia

---

[33]See *Tafseer Altabary for Sura Ahzab* 45/22 and *Tafseer Al-Baidawy* 386/4. There are many other examples.

Also:

> When Umar Ibn Alkhatab travelled in Medina...If he saw "Ama" or
> a slave girl, he would beat her with his Durra (a special type of stick)
> until the Hijab fell off and he would say: "How come the slave girls
> are trying to emulate the free women by wearing the Hijab!"
> – Tabakat Ibn Saad

As we can see, the *hijab* plays a role in the discrimination
against women. Contrary to what many claim, its purpose
is not "modesty" or to encourage observers to focus on a
Muslim woman's "personality". Its purpose, according to
the most authentic hadith books and interpretations, is to
create a society where "superior" free Muslim women are
distinguished from "inferior" slave women.

In Australia, the foremost Islamic cleric is Sheik Taj Din
al-Hilali. In 2006 he gave a sermon in which he analyzed
the notorious "Sydney Gang Rapes" – four women brutally
raped by a group of Muslim men. He complained that the
men received long jail sentences: "you get a judge without
mercy (*rahma*) and gives you 65 years." It was the victims'
fault: "...but the problem all began with who?" he asked.
He declared that the women "sway suggestively", wore
cosmetics and dressed immodestly. They were "weapons"
used by Satan to manipulate men. As if what he was saying
wasn't clear, he offered an analogy:

> If you take out uncovered meat and place it outside on the street, or
> in the garden or in the park, or in the backyard without a cover, and
> the cats come and eat it ... whose fault is it, the cats or the uncovered
> meat? ...The uncovered meat is the problem.... If she was in her room,
> in her home, in her hijab, no problem would have occurred.... It is
> said in the state of zina (adultery), the responsibility falls 90 per cent
> of the time on the woman. Why? Because she possesses the weapon of
> enticement (igraa).[34]

[34]Richard Kerbaj, "Muslim leader blames women for sex attacks", *The
Australian*, October 26, 2006, http://www.theaustralian.news.com.au/
story/0,20867,20646437-601,00.html

When young Muslims hear sermons like this it breeds hatred. We have noted that hatred is the first phase in constructing the jihadist mentality. Sadly, it also breeds hatred by women who wear the *hijab* for those who do not. My wife – who wore the *hijab* for years – used to think that uncovered women were "cheap" before she discarded it and began wearing ordinary modern dress.

Not only does the *hijab* foster gender discrimination in Islamic societies, but it fosters hatred for non-Muslim women who wear normal clothing. Many terrorist attacks take place in areas where Western women wear bathing suits or dance with men. Discotheques in Israel were a favorite target, as well as the infamous Bali nightclubs, in which 202 people were killed, 209 injured. Beaches in Egypt and Indonesia have been victimized by jihadist attacks, and there have been plots to bomb discos in London as well. The hatred of women who do not wear the *hijab* was a pivotal factor behind such attacks.

It cannot escape notice that the proliferation of the *hijab* is strongly correlated with increased terrorism. The *hijab* is on the one hand a sign of Salafist proliferation and on the other hand a factor that perpetuates it. Growth in terrorism to this extent has almost never stemmed from Muslim communities when the *hijab* was uncommon. Terrorism became much more frequent in such societies as Indonesia, Egypt, Algeria, and the UK – after the *hijab* became prevalent among Muslim women in those communities. The proliferation of the *hijab* preceded the increase in fundamentalism within Muslim communities in Kosovo as well. There, Islamic fundamentalism was a factor in fueling conflict between Muslims and Christians. It is true, also, in Iraq; terrorism was much more prevalent in the Sunni areas where the *hijab* is common (such as Al-Anbar) than in Sunni communities where the *hijab* is less frequently seen (e.g. among Sunni Kurds).

As the *hijab* becomes ubiquitous, young women are wearing it at progressively earlier ages. According to the hadiths, girls are only supposed to wear the *hijab* after puberty (to hide sexual attractiveness). The current trend of some Muslims to make young girls wear it may indicate a perverted way of thinking: when Muslim fathers require young girls to wear the *hijab*, it can imply these girls are viewed as sexually desirable enough to merit covering. Young Muslims – male and female – who grow up in this twisted atmosphere of Salafist gender oppression are the fodder for future jihadists.

Another form of mistreatment, polygamy, leads to phase two – suppression of conscience. This polygamy is not consensual. It does not matter how the wife feels about the additional woman, since 'Allah has permitted it and the Prophet practiced it'.

As with much else that is wrong with many Islamic societies, the oppression of women has deep roots in Islamic and especially Salafist writings. Salafism fuels the reactionary interpretations of scripture that justify oppression of women. In turn, the abuse of women plays a central role in desensitizing young Muslim men to violence. As we have mentioned earlier, desensitization to violence is one of the tactics that jihadists use to indoctrinate and train recruits. When a Muslim man becomes indifferent to women being beaten, maimed, or stoned to death, it is a much smaller step for him to commit acts of terrorism.

By now, many viewers have watched the videos on TV of Saudi Imams explaining the "humane" technique for beating a wife.[35] Doing so is sanctioned by a frequently cited passage in the Quran:

> *Men have authority over women because God has made the one superior to the other, and because they spend their wealth to maintain them. Good women are obedient. They guard their unseen parts because God has guarded them. As for those from whom you fear*

---

[35]The Middle East Media Research Institute, TV Monitor Project, "*Saudi Cleric Muhammad Al-'Arifi Explains Wife Beating in Islam to Young Muslims in a Ramadhan Show*", http://www.memritv.org/clip/en/1594.htm

disobedience, admonish them and send them to beds apart and beat them. Then if they obey you, take no further action against them. Surely God is high, supreme.

{Quran 4:34}

Wife beating leads to the third phase of jihadist indoctrination – the acceptance of violence.

As we have discussed earlier in this chapter, the failure of many Islamic societies to embrace modernity and teach values of true tolerance and respect for others has contributed to the development of the phenomenon of terrorism and Islamism. This failure partially stems from promoting a violent understanding of Islamic texts. Proper educational reforms are vital for the future success of the Islamic world and for the security of the whole world.

In the next chapter, we will deal with the mistakes of western societies that facilitated and even aggravated the proliferation and growth of Radical Islam.

Chapter 4:

The Failure of the West

Chapter 4: The Failure of the West

Lack of Reciprocity

Recently in the UK, a very expensive and widespread advertising campaign called "Islam is Peace" advocated "dialogue". Its ads are seen on TV, in print, on billboards, and on city buses. The second point of its five-point plan is "To create dialogue – to create permanent channels of dialogue and debate between the Muslim community and the rest of Britain, ensuring that your voice is always in the mainstream media."[36] If the campaign wants "debate", then why does it not ask for the debate to be in the mainstream media and not just the Muslim "voice"? Is this a dialogue or really a monologue that the campaign seeks? It is both intellectually dishonest as well as a sign of weakness when non-Muslims are a passive audience in this dialogue and Muslims alone voice their opinions. The "Islam is Peace" campaign is part of a larger problem – the lack of reciprocity. Westerners criticize their own societies with great gusto, but rarely their Muslim communities. Muslims criticize Western communities, but rarely their own.

This isn't dialogue. It is intellectual and moral absurdity.

When Western women leaders visit Islamic countries, they respectfully wear the *hijab*. Do traditional Muslim women wear jeans and t-shirts when they visit Western countries? Do they go to the beach and wear a normal woman's bathing suit? The lack of reciprocity would be unacceptable even if the *hijab* did not represent a division between free and slave women and did not play a key role in gender apartheid.

---

[36]Islam is Peace, http://www.islamispeace.org.uk/
See Spencer's fine critique of the Islam is Peace campaign:
Robert Spencer, comment on "Spencer on Islam Is Peace campaign: "Be Creative"", *JihadWatch*, comment posted December 3, 2007, http://www.jihadwatch.org/archives/019006.php

Similarly, Muslims were up in arms when Pope Benedict XVI cited a passage from a 1391 tract which criticized Islam. Even though the citation was made in the context of a larger lecture, Muslim riots erupted around the world. In order to quell the unrest, the Pope visited Turkey and prayed in a mosque, facing Mecca.[37] Yet if dialogue was the goal, why didn't Muslims show the Pope reciprocal gestures of respect? Muslim scholars could have prayed in the Vatican and signed themselves with the cross.

In 2007, the management of the Empire State Building in New York City decided to illuminate the building in green to honor the end of Ramadan and the Islamic holiday of Eid. There would be nothing wrong with this decision if Muslims reciprocated the honor. But given the state of current Islamic teaching, which advocates that Sharia replace secular law, and given the 3000 that died on 9/11 at the hands of Islamists, it is not only inappropriate but is seen by jihadists as a victory.

In the UK, the town of Derby proudly displayed a statue of a wild boar from 1840 to 1942, when the sculpture was decapitated by a German bomb. Recently, the city planned to replace the statue with another one of a boar, but the local Muslim community became enraged, claiming it was offensive.[38] In another incident, the UK town of Dudley passed a law forbidding workers to have figurines of pigs on their desks. Apparently, a Muslim employee complained that such desk ornaments offended his faith. According to then-Councilor of Dudley, Mahbubur Rahman, the law is "tolerance and acceptance of their beliefs and understanding".[39] But where does this "tolerance" end and

---

[37] I have tremendous respect for Pope Benedict for showing such genuine desire for peace.

[38] "Arboretum", *The Derby Gripe*, http://www.derbygripe.co.uk/arbor.htm, accessed on December 27. 2007

[39] Mark Steyn, "Making a pigs ear of defending democracy", *The Telegraph*, April 10, 2005, http://www.telegraph.co.uk/opinion/main.jhtml?xml=/opinion/2005/10/04/do0402.xml

why does it only extend in one direction? If some Christians complained that wearing the Islamic scarf was offensive to them, would the same decision makers ask Muslim women to stop wearing it? Elsewhere, the phenomenon can be much more severe. In Egypt, veiled women stormed an art museum crying "Infidels, Infidels" and attempted to destroy three works of art. The reason: a sculptor had violated a *fatwa* issued by the Grand Mufti of Cairo, which banned images of living beings.[40] When Salafism has its way, the results are depressing and irreparable. It came as no surprise that the Taliban destroyed the historically priceless Buddhist statues of Bamyan by dynamiting them.

If Muslims objected to pig figurines and the statue of a boar, it leads one to wonder what the breaking point is for Westerners. What if Muslims found Christmas trees offensive; should they be removed or banned? If Muslims declared that women's' rights are offensive or that prohibiting slavery is insulting to their faith, should we surrender to their sensitivities as a matter of religious tolerance? Indeed, it is strange that Christianity is constantly assaulted by Western progressives, both in word and in the actions of organizations such as the American Civil Liberties Union (ACLU). The ACLU worked diligently to remove a monument of the Ten Commandments from an Alabama courthouse, a "victory" disapproved of by 77% of Americans. But the ACLU has not worked nearly as hard, if at all, to stop Islamic infiltrations into secular institutions. The ACLU has said nothing about the plan to install Islamic foot baths in restrooms at the Minnesota Community and Technical College – a taxpayer-funded, public institution. School president Phil Davies claimed that the Islamic foot baths are a sign of tolerance and "hospitality", but insisted that departmental Christmas cards not exhibit "any sign of favoring one religion", adding, "As we head into the holiday season ... all public offices

---

[40]Harry de Quetteville, "Statue attack fuels fears of an Islamist Egypt", *The Telegraph*, June 18, 2006, http://www.telegraph.co.uk/news/main.jhtml?xml=/news/2006/06/18/wegypt18.xml

and areas should refrain from displays that may represent to our students, employees or the public that the college is promoting any particular religion."[41] Apparently, the school president does not see any contradiction. Muslim footbaths do not promote a particular religion, but Christmas cards do.

I cannot help but recall the way *Jamaa Islamiya* gradually dominated our medical school. They asked for permission to build a prayer room, then added a library; next came Salafist sermons before lectures and angry demonstrations to prevent music. We in the West are experiencing a failure of limits. It is a vicious cycle: the more we surrender, the more Islamists demand, the more we surrender. Perhaps democracy itself is offensive; perhaps universities should be governed by Sharia. Everything is possible unless we insist on respecting religious freedom within the bounds of constitutions – something the ACLU selectively and pedantically enforces. This one-directional, schizophrenic desire to appease Islamists leads to absurdity. Nowhere was it seen more clearly than when Muslim cab drivers at the Minneapolis airport refused to accept blind passengers with guide dogs. It was only with great difficulty that they were compelled to do so.

There are hundreds of such examples – underreported, over-reported, or badly reported – and they show why the problem of violent Islam seems endless. One of the strengths of the West is its tolerance and freedom. Unfortunately, Islamists see examples such as these as capitulation and weakness. If human beings are to respect one another's cultures, it must be bi-directional. The current environment of one-way appeasement is generating the opposite outcome.

---

[41]Robert Spencer, comment on "Minnesota college to install facilities for Muslim daily prayers", *DhimmiWatch*, April 12, 2007, http://www.jihad-watch.org/dhimmiwatch/archives/016020.php

Political Concessions

Apologies

Normally, issuing an apology for making a mistake is an act that is respected by civilized people. However, when an enemy considers the apology as a sign of weakness and thus becomes more vicious, one must think twice before apologizing again. One of the best examples of this phenomenon was the rioting over the cartoons of Prophet Muhammad. The cartoons were published in Denmark by *Jyllands-Posten* magazine on the 30th of September 2005. Until the 30th of January 2006 there were virtually no violent demonstrations on the "Muslim street." This translates to four months of relative peace. When the magazine issued an apology for the publication of the cartoons on the 31st, within a few days violent demonstrations erupted throughout the Islamic world. In other words, if the magazine had not apologized, the violent demonstrations would probably not have occurred. This dynamic illustrates a mentality that is totally alien to Westerners. Islamist minds react violently only after they feel their opponent has exhibited weakness. The more they see concessions, the more violently they attempt to gain them.

Another example that illustrates this bizarre attribute of the Islamist mind is the reaction of jihadists to anti-war demonstrations in US. Jihadists perceive demonstrations against the war in Iraq to be a sign of disunity among infidel enemies. Thus, such demonstrations very likely prompt Jihadists to intensify terrorism efforts. One of the worst weeks in Iraq in terms of civilian casualties occurred immediately after the anti-war demonstrations led by Jane Fonda. More than a thousand innocents were killed in that week alone. I have no doubt that Jane Fonda and many of the demonstrators did not mean to facilitate the deaths of civilians, but the reality is that their demonstrations likely contributed to the loss of more innocent lives than would have occurred otherwise. Such demonstrations have served only to impede and delay victory in Iraq. If terrorists saw that Americans were demonstrating against them – instead of demonstrating against their own country – they would have felt defeated at the 'mental level' and the number of terrorist attacks would have declined. It is equally ironic that Leftist demonstrations on the one hand impede victory in Iraq and at the same time Leftists blame all the failures in Iraq on the US government. This does not mean that there were no tactical mistakes or wrong decisions in the post-war planning in Iraq. But the solution is not to demonstrate against your country in time of war; the solution is to encourage morale and to develop new tactics to win that war.

Islamists will never come out and say, "We are being appeased and that gives us courage to attack". Thus, critics will argue that any correlation between violence and concessions, in the absence of supporting jihadist statements of this type, is circumstantial. Yet the correlation is statistically striking. After the publications, in 2005, of the Muhammad cartoons by a Danish newspaper, Muslims riots started in earnest only after the paper issued an apology.

Unwise Immigration Policies

In 2003, Muslims were permitted to build a controversial mosque in Grenada, Spain. The Spanish have a particularly sensitive history regarding the Islamic conquest, because the nation was dominated by the Moors for centuries. The BBC gushed that the mosque "heralds a new dawn for the faith in Europe"[42] and mosque spokesman Abdel Haqq Salaberria agreed, "It will act as a focal point for the Islamic revival in Europe." The reader will recall what the words "Islamic revival" meant in my Egyptian medical school. Construction of this historic mosque under these circumstances – especially after 9/11 – was perceived by Islamists as a Western

---

[42]"Mosque signals Muslims' return to Spain", *BBC News*, July 10, 2003, http://news.bbc.co.uk/2/hi/europe/3055377.stm

concession, even a retreat, and prompted more violence. Almost one year later, on 11 March 2004, the Madrid subways were bombed by Al Qaeda, killing 191 and wounding 2050. Initially, it was believed that the Basque separatist group ETA was responsible. The Spanish demonstrated in millions against the Basque group, but when the truth emerged that Al Qaeda was responsible (i.e. Muslims), the demonstrations stopped at once. Apparently, self criticism is fine, but criticism of others is taboo. It is widely believed that Spanish Prime Minister Jose Aznar and his Partido Popular lost the general elections three days later because of the attacks. Aznar supported President Bush and the war in Iraq. The new Prime Minister, liberal Jose Zapatero, withdrew the Spanish forces. It was a significant victory for Islamists on every level: they derived recognition from building a controversial mosque and then compelled Spanish voters to install an appeasing government. However, withdrawal from Iraq did not protect Spain from being the target of another Islamist plot. Later in 2004, 32 Islamists were arrested for planning to bomb the National Court in Madrid. It does not matter whether Westerners believe they are making a concession; it matters only that Islamists perceive it to be one.

Yet participation in Iraq is not the reason Islamists attack and has little bearing on Islamist recruitment. In 2004, French Muslims rioted in large numbers in 274 French cities. The riots lasted twenty days, during which 8973 cars were firebombed, 126 police and firefighters were injured, and one person slain. Damage was estimated at 200M Euros.[43] A smaller repeat of the riots occurred in 2007. The media, the French government, academics, and Islamic groups made every effort to blame factors other than Islamism. Rioters are still referred to as "youths", as underprivileged immigrants, or as victims of segregation. These apologists did not realize that the Algerian Islamists were not segregated inside

---

[43]Wikipedia contributors, "2005 civil unrest in France," *Wikipedia, The Free Encyclopedia*, http://en.wikipedia.org/w/index.php?title=2005_civil_un-rest_in_France&oldid=177451138 (accessed December 21, 2007).

Algeria, yet they engaged in acts of terrorism that ended the lives of 200,000 innocents. In view of this fact, it is hard to believe that segregation was the cause of the problem. Those factors certainly played a role, despite the fact that the rioters received government benefits and enjoyed a standard of living typically much higher than can be found in their ancestral homelands. But the reality is that rioters often chanted "Allahu Akhbar" and that Islamist incitement fueled the rioting. The irony is that the French made every effort to appease the Islamic world. The French government never supported the war in Iraq and never sent troops. French political leaders criticized the "cowboy" foreign policy of President Bush at every opportunity. It scored them no points. What is more, as Bat Ye'or describes in her seminal work, *Eurabia: The Euro Arab Axis*, the existence of unassimilated Muslim enclaves – called *banlieu* in France – originated in large part from explicit non-assimilation agreements between the European Union and Islamic countries.

The real cause of the riots in France could have been discovered using straightforward statistical logic. If non-Muslims living in France under the same socio-economic circumstances participated in the riots on a percentage basis *equal* to their percentage in the suburbs, then it could be concluded that the problem was likely related to socio-economic circumstances. On the other hand, if non-Muslim participation in the riots was relatively less than their proportion among young non-Muslims living in identical circumstances, then the problem is more likely to be Islamism-related.

One must ask a few basic questions: Why don't we hear about violence occurring to the same degree among other minorities who live in the West? Why is there a tendency towards violence among people who follow certain forms of religious teaching? Can it simply be a coincidence?

Unwise immigration policies are a core problem in many democratic nations. They have enabled jihadists to enter secular democratic states and propagate violent Salafist beliefs. Since the 1970s, Canada has allowed explosive rates of immigration from Islamic states. Immigrants are treated well, receiving health care and welfare benefits. Like the French, the Canadian government did not support the Iraq war and did not send troops. Nevertheless, in June 2006 authorities broke-up a 17-person Islamic terrorist cell. The conspiracy had plotted to assassinate the prime minister and blow up a variety of government targets. It had accumulated three metric tons of ammonium nitrate – 1600 lbs more than was used by Timothy McVeigh.

In Britain, preachers of hate such as Abu-Hamza El-Masry were allowed for decades to teach young Muslims. Ultimately, the UK experienced the subway bombings on 7 July 2005. The terrorists who conducted these barbaric acts were home-grown; they were born, reared and educated in the UK. The authorities in the UK claimed that these young Muslims turned into jihadists because they had each visited Pakistan. The authorities simply could not believe that a child who was educated in Britain could become a suicide bomber – that a child could be inculcated with Islamist ideology right in their own back yard. The knee-jerk reaction was to blame another country for it. If years of education in the UK were not enough to protect young Muslims from becoming jihadists against a few months spent in an Islamic country, then the UK needs to question the effectiveness of their whole educational system.

What the authorities in the UK did not comprehend was that "physical" training camps are not as important as "ideological" training camps – one does not need to attend "physical" training camps in Pakistan when ideological training camps in British mosques already teach hatred. Young Muslims do not need to travel to faraway places to receive violent indoctrination. On 7 January 2007, the *Observer* revealed an undercover investigation that exposed disturbing evidence of Islamic extremism at several important British mosques and Islamic institutions, including an organization praised by the Prime Minister. Secret video footage revealed Muslim preachers exhorting followers to prepare for jihad, to beat girls who did not wear the Hijab, and to create a "state within a state". Many of the preachers were found linked to Saudi Wahhabis, who fund a number of Britain's leading Islamic institutions. According to *The Times*, books which called for the beheading of lapsed Muslims, for constraining women indoors, and for prohibiting interfaith marriage were being sold inside some of these mosques. If we allow this form of teaching to infiltrate the mind of young Muslims, why should we be surprised that home-grown Islamic terrorism develops in the West?

Quiet Scandinavia is quiet no longer. In Denmark, 75% of all rapes are committed by immigrants, almost entirely Muslim. In Norway, Muslims constitute 2% of the population and, as with Denmark, nearly the whole of the immigrant community. In 2001, 65% of all rapes in Norway were committed by immigrants.[44] Among Norwegian immigrants there is a severe problem with arranged, usually forced marriages. In an article for the Christian Science Monitor, Bruce Bawer has noted:

> *There are, naturally, no statistics on forced marriages in Norway. But HRS's [Oslo-based Human Rights Service] figures for henteekteskap, or "fetching marriages" - in which one spouse is "fetched" from the other's ancestral country - are startling. Between 1996 and 2001, 82 percent of Norwegian daughters of Moroccan immigrants who got married, married Moroccan citizens. For Norwegian daughters of Pakistani immigrants, the corresponding rate was 76 percent.[45]*

In Holland, measures have been introduced to curb importation of spouses. There, artist Theo Van Gogh was murdered for his film *Submission* by Muslims enraged at

---

[44]Mark Steyn, "Battered Westerner Syndrome inflicted by myopic Muslim defenders", *Jewish World Review*, August 23, 2002, http://www.jewishworldreview.com/0802/steyn1.asp

[45]Bruce Bawer, "A Problem with Muslim Enclaves", *The Christian Science Monitor*, June 30, 2003, http://www.csmonitor.com/2003/0630/p09s01-coop.html

the Dutchman's stand against Islamism. Similarly, Ayan Hirsi Ali received constant death threats in response to her criticisms of Islam, and was forced to live in hiding while serving as a member of the Dutch parliament. In 2004, Dutch intelligence published a report, *From Dawa to Jihad*, in which they noted that there are 50,000 potential jihadists in Holland, that the number of members in jihadist groups is growing, that Holland is ill-prepared to manage the problem, and that the Islamic community showed low resistance to Islamist infiltration.[46]

It would be exhausting to itemize every single example of poor immigration policies, but suffice it to say that similar problems have occurred in Sweden, Belgium, Germany, Thailand, Australia, and elsewhere. When properly implemented, immigration is a good thing. Immigrants contribute monumentally to the success of a nation – they are essential. It is only when nations fail to be judicious about whom they let in that the problems begin to develop, and once they do develop, they can be astonishingly difficult to solve.

Weak Military Responses

Yet the failure of modern democratic nations lies not only in words and domestic policies, but in geo-political decisions and military responses to Islamic terror. Foreign policies have at times been disastrously wrong-headed. As for military responses, they have typically been absent, half-hearted, un-thorough, or excessively delayed. In saying this, it is important to distinguish the weak responses of US foreign policy regarding terrorism from the Leftist contention that American foreign policy is an understandable motivation for Islamism. Islamism and Terrorism are never – under any

---

[46]Manfred Gerstenfeld, "Radical Islam in The Netherlands: A Case Study of a Failed European Policy", *Jerusalem Issue Brief*, Vol. 4, No. 14, Jerusalem Center for Public Affairs, http://www.jcpa.org/brief/brief004-14.htm

circumstances – natural, logical, or justified. The question is not whether American involvement in the Middle East is the source of Islamic terror, but that American involvement has not aggressively attacked the problem of terror. It must also be said that when we analyze US failures to confront Islamism, we must avoid partisanship. Administrations of various ideological stripes have made grievous errors, and if we are to learn from our mistakes we must be objective. Islamism and terror have been permitted to grow and fester throughout the world while Western nations juggled political and economic priorities which were deemed more important. It was only on 9/11 that free societies realized that Islamism is an existential threat. The festering is not a recent development – it has intensified continuously since the 1970s, through various shifts in Western leadership.

Perhaps the first event that inaugurated the looming catastrophe was President Jimmy Carter's management of the Iranian Revolution and the resulting hostage crisis. When the Shaw was deposed, Carter refused him a visa to get medical treatment in the US (in contrast, Iranian President Mahmoud Ahmedinejad was permitted to speak in New York in 2007). This rejection sent a diplomatic message that America was a fair-weather friend, an untrustworthy partner in any endeavor. Who would not be wary of depending on America when agreements and governments are jettisoned so easily? The problem, however, was not merely that Carter accepted Khomeini's Islamist regime, but that he welcomed it. Carter wasn't too concerned when Khomeini announced, "Do not use this term, 'democratic'. That is the Western style". Despite these ominous words and Khomeini's reign of terror that killed hundreds of leaders of the old regime, Carter lifted the embargo on arms sales to Iran. Carter's National Security Advisor, Zbigniew Brzezinski, pushed through a plan that was founded on using Islamic nations as a bulwark against Soviet expansion and which therefore sought close relations with them across the board. Leftists overseas, in both Iran and in the international community, sought to disrupt this rapprochement with America, and at their instigation, the

US embassy in Teheran was taken over, its members held hostage.

According to columnist and security analyst Amir Taheri, Khomeini expected a swift and decisive response from the US, but Carter equivocated. Carter's representative at the United Nations, Andrew Young, referred to Khomeini as "a 20th-century saint" and begged the ayatollah to show "magnanimity and compassion."[47] When he saw that no serious reaction was forthcoming from America, Khomeini allowed the crisis to last an almost unthinkable 444 days. During that time, Carter thought it best to conduct a limited covert military operation to rescue all 63 hostages in the heart of a city of approximately 5 million inhabitants. The operation, managed personally by Carter over the telephone, met with disaster long before its participants reached Teheran, when helicopters encountered mechanical failures and dust storms. The mission could not be kept from world TV audiences as videos of crashed helicopters were broadcast. American humiliation deepened and Islamist exhilaration exploded.

The hostages were released one hour after President Ronald Reagan was inaugurated. There are many who say that the hostages were released because Carter had brokered a deal with the Iranians, in which the US agreed to unfreeze $8 billion of Iranian assets and swore never to intervene in Iranian affairs. In a 2001 retrospective, CBS News sneered that it was the Reagan's "Lucky Day".[48] But an examination of Reagan's campaign speeches and his firm actions as governor shows clearly that the Mullahs had something to fear from a Reagan administration. In Reagan's acceptance speech for the Republican nomination, he declared:

---

[47] Amir Taheri, "America can't do a thing", *New York Post*, November 2, 2004, available online at http://www.benadorassociates.com/article/8781

[48] "Reagan's Lucky Day – Iranian Hostage Crisis Helped The Great Communicator To Victory", *CBS News*, January 21, 2001, http://www.cbsnews.com/stories/2001/01/19/iran/main265499.shtml

Adversaries large and small test our will and seek to confound our resolve, but we are given weakness when we need strength, vacillation when the times demand firmness.

The Carter Administration lives in a world of make-believe – every day, drawing up a response to that day's problems – troubles, regardless of what happened yesterday and what'll happen tomorrow.

But you and I live in a real world, where disasters are overtaking our nation without any real response from Washington. This is make-believe, self-deceit and, above all, transparent hypocrisy.[49]

That Reagan's assertions were accurate was confirmed, even at the time, by political adversaries who agreed with him. For example, Democratic Senator Patrick Moynihan stated that Carter is "unable to distinguish between our friends and our enemies, he has essentially adopted our enemies' view of the world."[50]

Reagan was able to distinguish friend from foe, but unfortunately, while Reagan performed well in fostering the collapse of the Soviet Union, his record against Islamism was unsatisfactory. His troubles started with the US involvement in Lebanon in 1982, after he ordered the Marines to return and help the multi-national force quell the conflict. On 18 April 1983, the US embassy in Beirut was destroyed by a suicide bomber, killing 57. The terrorist group Islamic Jihad[51] took responsibility, and significantly, this particular attack was backed by Iran. In a telephone interview, the group claimed:

---

[49]Ronald Reagan, "1980 Republican National Convention Address", *American Rhetoric*, http://www.americanrhetoric.com/speeches/ronaldreagan1980rnc.htm, accessed December 3, 2007

[50]Noemie Emery, "The Muse of Malaise", *The Weekly Standard*, July 5, 2004, http://www.weeklystandard.com/Content/Public/Articles/000/000/004/271qgfin.asp?pg=1

[51]Here we see the word *jihad* again. This group is not to be confused with both the Palestinian and Egyptian groups of the same name, which are Sunni.

This is part of the Iranian revolution's campaign against imperialist targets throughout the world. We shall keep striking at any imperialist presence in Lebanon, including the international force.[52]

We can see in this statement the Leftist boilerplate of Imperialism that jihadists mouth to disguise their Islamist agenda. International forces were deployed to Lebanon to stop the violence, not conquer the country. Yet the peacekeeping mission did have a flaw: by attempting to "quell" Islamist violence, it sought to cure the symptoms of Islamism and not the disease itself – a disease that had been growing rapidly in disparate locations around the globe. The US responded five months later, when it fired 368 artillery rounds in support of the Lebanese Air Force – an underwhelming response.[53] Four days later, on 23 October, the Marine barracks were bombed. The death toll was staggering – 241 Marines were killed in the attack. It is not entirely clear which Islamic group perpetrated it – several claimed responsibility. The Free Islamic Revolutionary Movement was able to identify the bombers, but later investigations suggested that another organization backed by Iran was responsible – Hezbollah. After some indecision as to how to respond, the reaction of the multi-national force, which included American forces, was to withdraw entirely from Lebanon. The attack on both the embassy and the

Marines went unpunished, and jihadists knew they could act with impunity. Once again, America had accomplished nothing and had made the problem of Islamism much worse.

[52]Wikipedia contributors, "1983 United States Embassy bombing," *Wikipedia, The Free Encyclopedia*, http://en.wikipedia.org/w/index.php?title=1983_United_States_Embassy_bombing&oldid=172880941 (accessed December 21, 2007).

[53]Lieutenant Colonel John E. Kasperski, USMC and Major Benjamin D. Crockett, USA, "U.S. Involvement in Lebanon, 1982-84: An Analysis of Failures to Determine National Interests and Apply the Elements of Power", *Joint Forces Staff College, Joint and Combined Warfighting School – Intermediate*, March 5, 2004, http://www.jfsc.ndu.edu/current_students/documents_policies/documents/jca_cca_awsp/US_Involvemement_Lebanon_4-7-04.doc

On 12 December 1983, an Iraqi terrorist organization known as Al-Dawa, in conjunction with Islamic Jihad, set off a number of bombs in Kuwait that foreshadowed that modus operandi of Al Qaeda – simultaneity, suicide bombers, and close coordination. American and French embassies were hit, and attempts were made on the airport, an oil refinery, an electric plant, and a US corporation. There were six fatalities – a small number – which resulted from the driver of a truck failing to approach the chancellery building. The US did very little to retaliate, but the Kuwaitis were apparently surprised, and commenced a massive round-up of suspects, resulting in the imprisonment of Al-Dawa members. In reaction to this imprisonment, Hezbollah took 30 Westerners hostage in Lebanon, including several Americans. The Islamists' war against America had been festering for many years, but Western leaders failed to recognize its potential and did virtually nothing to stop its malignant growth.

As we skip ahead in time to the Clinton Administration, the debate over his record against Islamism becomes much more partisan and much more heated. In a September 2006 interview, award-winning FoxNews host Chris Wallace (a registered Democrat) asked Clinton about allegations from the 9/11 Commission Report about concerns over his management of counter-terrorism. Viewers themselves, according to Wallace, had written in large numbers with the same questions. Clinton responded:

> *I will answer all those things on the merits, but first I want to talk about the context in which this arises. I'm being asked this on the Fox network. ABC just had a right-wing conservative runnin' their little pathway[54] to 9/11.*

---

[54]David L. Cunningham, "The Path to 9/11", available at Amazon.com: http://www.amazon.com/Path-9-11-Harvey-Keitel/dp/B00005JPHZ/ref=sr_1_1?ie=UTF8&s=dvd&qid=1197606392&sr=1-1

He blamed "the right-wingers who are attacking me now" and told Wallace, "you've got that little smirk on your face and you think you're so clever."[55]

Citizens have demanded explanations for why the 9/11 attacks were not prevented. In response, various former members of the CIA have written books on the subject; retired generals and administration officials have done the same. Some admonish Clinton; others have attempted to defend his track record. The 9/11 Commission Report is probably our best guide to the failures, despite critics who dispute its conclusions and the evidence presented. Underlying the rancorous debate is the fact that much information is simply classified or unknown, and that ulterior motives play a role in suppressing facts. Therefore, it is helpful to step back from the low-level blaming – between Clinton, Congressional Republicans, the CIA, partisans on both sides – and look at the big picture.

As one might expect, that picture is bleak. In 1991, the African nation of Somalia became embroiled in a civil war between Islamic warlords. Millions of innocents were caught in the crossfire. Somali agricultural production was destroyed leading to wide scale starvation. The international community began to send large quantities of food and supplies, but up to 80% of these were stolen by the warring factions. 300,000 Somalis lost their lives to famine, and as the humanitarian crisis deepened, a multinational force was sent in to protect the distribution of aid. As time passed, military operations were directed against some of these warlords who were interfering with food distribution. Then, in 3-4 October 1993, a coalition force consisting mostly of US troops, but also of Pakistani and Malaysian soldiers, was sent against the Somali militia headed by Muhammad Farrah Aidid in

---

[55]"Transcript: William Jefferson Clinton on 'FOX News Sunday'", *FoxNews*, September 26, 2006, http://www.foxnews.com/story/0,2933,215397,00. html
As of this writing, his video is available on YouTube: http://www.youtube. com/watch?v=WYNI5RPOlp4

the capital of Mogadishu. Over the city, two Blackhawk helicopters were shot down and isolated. The troops in the helicopters were forced to fight their way out, and in the process, 18 American servicemen were killed and 73 were wounded. Estimates vary for Somali casualties, but combined militia and civilian casualties are believed to lie in the range of 1000-1500.

The American response, after uproar at home, was to promise a withdrawal of US forces by April 1994. Once again, Islamists won a propaganda victory against the US. Jihadists saw the "Great Satan" as a paper tiger lacking resolve and staying power. Equally as frustrating, evidence is very strong that Osama bin Laden was involved in training Aidid's forces. It is astonishing, but while the American government has had incredible difficulty locating bin Laden, CNN reporter Peter Bergen was able interview him in 1997. In this exchange, bin Laden told Bergen that he had trained and financed Aidad's forces. Thus, the American withdrawal from Somalia was not only a victory for Islamists in general, but specifically, a triumph for Al Qaeda.

At the same time that the trouble in Somalia was playing out, the first attempt to destroy the World Trade Centers occurred in 1993. Six people were killed and 1042 were injured after a truck bomb carrying 1500 lbs of urea nitrate was detonated in the parking garage of tower one. Four Islamic terrorists were quickly rounded up and convicted and two more were convicted in 1997. The suspects were apprehended so quickly in part because an Egyptian army colonel, Emad Salem (who claimed to have informed the FBI of the plot in 1992), was able to identify the suspects. Al Qaeda was linked to the attack – the group was financed by Al Qaeda member Khalid Sheikh Muhammed. Members were also eventually connected to Sheikh Abdel Rahman, who was then indicted and convicted of conspiracy to commit terror.

Yet, other than apprehending some of the perpetrators, the US took no other important action. It treated terrorism as a law enforcement problem rather than an ideological threat that needed to be eradicated. Terrorist organizations and infrastructures did not otherwise suffer, and state sponsors of terror were not made to pay the price.

The straw that broke the camel's back came in 1998, when simultaneous explosions rocked US embassies in Tanzania and Kenya. In Dar es Salaam, the attack killed 11 and wounded 85, while in Nairobi, 212 were killed and at least 4000 injured. The attacks were once again linked to Al Qaeda and for the first time, bin Laden (at last) was placed on the FBI's most-wanted list. Al Qaeda by then had been murdering Americans for years and the time was ripe for some form of full-scale confrontation. Unfortunately, the US response was once again tepid. Cruise missiles were launched at terrorist training camps in Afghanistan and at a pharmaceutical factory in Sudan. This weak response to the embassy bombings merely confirmed to jihadists that America is a "Paper Tiger" and encouraged Al Qaeda to prepare for the 9/11 attacks.

The inadequate American answer to terrorism can be likened to an insufficient use of antibiotics to treat an infection: it does not cure the disease and at the same time it allows the emergence of resistant strains. The same applies to military responses. One must either conduct them in a potent and focused manner or not engage the enemy at all. Using insufficient power aggravates the problem because it reveals to jihadists their enemy's constraints and vulnerabilities. Even if they experience some casualties, jihadists will seize upon the weakness and intensify their terrorism efforts. Had the US administration responded with an iron fist, the probability of 9/11 happening would have been much less. Preventive military measures are vital to protect the US from further attacks by Al Qaeda. Destroying Bin Laden after the attacks in Kenya and Tanzania was a national security obligation.

According to an NBC report,[56] in the fall of 2000 an unmanned Predator drone snapped photos of what looks to be bin Laden, and what many intelligence analysts believe is bin Laden, at an Afghanistan facility. It is not clear why the US did not act. One CIA member said that the White House wanted bin Laden alive. Others contend that the Clinton administration was weakened by scandal and couldn't muster support for an attack. One general complained that military preparedness was insufficient for such an attack. Regardless of the reason or whom to blame, the outcome was that bin Laden survived to perpetrate 9/11.

America has been the victim of Islamic terrorism since the 1970s. Attacks have been unremitting and devastating; before 9/11 we witnessed the destruction of embassies, jetliners, ships, discothèques, airline counters, and barracks; we've seen peacekeeping forces attacked and ambassadors held hostage. During that time, America failed to understand Islamism. It treated terrorism as a criminal problem instead of an ideological one. Over a period of thirty years, over five administrations, the problem intensified. Since 9/11, to the credit of both the Bush administration and the intelligence services, there has not been an Islamic terrorist attack on US soil. Globally, however, the problem continues, and of course, the US is still at great risk.

The Collapse of the "Progressive" Movement

Today we constantly hear members of the multicultural Left issue politically correct justifications for Islamic terror. They have apologized for it and even supported it. The halls of academia are saturated with such injunctions, and the media promulgates it daily. The battle against Islamism and Islamic terror would have been difficult enough had modern, free people been united against it. Unfortunately, the statements

---

[56]Lisa Meyers, "Osama bin Laden: missed opportunities", *MSNBC Nightly News*, March 17, 2004, http://www.msnbc.msn.com/id/4540958/

and actions of large swaths of the Left have paved the way for Islamist barbarity. The examples are so numerous and the problem sufficiently complex as to make only a general outline possible in this book. Here, as a case study, I will evaluate some of the views of religion-writer Karen Armstrong.

Karen Armstrong

Armstrong is an exceptionally representative example of multicultural revisionism and moral backsliding. A former nun who now bills herself as a "freelance monotheist", she writes consistently about Islam and has become a celebrity among multiculturalists and especially, the media. Salon.com has hailed her as "arguably the most lucid, wide-ranging and consistently interesting religion writer today."[57]

In a 2002 PBS interview, Armstrong acknowledged that Islamic textbooks need improvement, but insinuates that Christian Sunday school books are just as bad,

> *Christians have got to change their textbooks. I'm still shocked by the way the Pharisees are presented in some school textbooks, giving children a very distorted notion of Judaism.*

Do Christian textbooks advocate the killing of Jews and the annihilation of Israel? Do they brand Jews the sons of apes and swine? Can't Armstrong differentiate between events that happened in the past and the Islamic books that currently promote killing Jews and dehumanizing them in our modern times?

Islam is "profoundly in tune with the whole American and western ethos" and

> *The heart of Islam beats with the heart of the American people. The passion that Islam has for equality – Islam is one of the most egalitarian religions I know and has always lived out its egalitarianism. It's at its best historically when it has had egalitarian*

[57]Dave Welch, "Karen Armstrong, Turn, Turn, Turn", *Powell's Books*, March 20, 2004, http://www.powells.com/authors/armstrong.html

forms of government, and [it is] unhappy with authoritarian forms of government, as it has now. That's one of the reasons Islam is unhappy, because it has a lot of despots and bad government and tyrannical government, some of which are supported by the United States and the West generally.

This is a gross distortion of both history and modern reality. It is true that Islam, at least in theory, is not supposed to make distinctions among believers. But it makes hugely non-egalitarian distinctions between believers and non-believers. Non-believers in Islamic societies are known as dhimmis. They were forced to pay the *jizya* and live as second-class citizens. This form of Islamic teaching is not just a historical reference but is currently what all sources of Sharia advocate. The egalitarianism she speaks of, if it ever existed, does not explain why dhimmis used to live under extreme discrimination under the Islamic Caliphate. The following were the conditions to which non-Muslims were subjected as decreed by the second Islamic Caliph, Umar Ibn Al-Khatab.

Al-Uhda Al-Umareia

Christians shall not build, in cities or in their neighborhood, new monasteries, Churches, convents, or monks' cells, nor shall they repair, by day or by night, such of them as fall in ruins or are situated in the quarters of the Muslims.

Christians shall keep their gates wide open for passersby and travelers. They shall give board and lodging to all Muslims who pass their way for three days.

Christians shall not give shelter in their churches or in their dwellings to any spy, nor hide him from the Muslims.

Christians shall not teach the Quran to their children.[58]

---

[58]Because Christians are considered unclean in the view of many Muslims.

Christians shall not manifest their religion publicly nor convert any Muslim to it. They shall not prevent any of their kin from entering Islam if they wish it.[59]

Christians shall show respect toward the Muslims, and they shall rise from their seats when Muslims wish to sit on them.

Christians shall not seek to resemble the Muslims by imitating any of their garments such as the Qalansuwa, the turban, footwear, or the parting of the hair. They shall not speak as Muslims do, nor shall they adopt their kunyas (nicknames).[60]

Christians shall not mount on saddles, nor shall they gird swords nor bear any kind of arms nor carry them on their persons.

Christians shall not engrave Arabic inscriptions on Muslims' seals.

Christians shall not sell fermented drinks.

Christians shall always dress in the same way wherever they may be, and they shall bind the Zunar (kind of belts) round their waists.

Christians shall not display their crosses or their books in the roads or markets of the Muslims. They shall use only clappers in their churches very softly. Christians shall not raise their voices while crying when following their dead.[61]

Is this what Armstrong calls "egalitarianism"?

She goes on:

People who talk about the need for Islam to have a reformation, "as we did" in the 16th century, show a great ignorance of Islam and the Protestant Reformation. Islam has had a constant series of

---

[59]At the same time, Muslims can convert Christians to Islam and may kill any Muslim who converts to Christianity by Redda (Apostasy-related) Law.

[60]Because Muslims look at Christians as inferior to them so, in their view, the inferior is not allowed to emulate the superior in his dress or name. This mirrors the Islamic teaching that slave girls are not allowed to wear the *hijab* while free women must.

[61]Raising the voice in a special manner and uttering special expressions to communicate grief is a part of Egyptian culture since the time of pharaohs. It is pre-Islamic, as it were.

reformations; you can trace most of them right back to the 13th, 14th century, even before. They went back to the basics, got rid of all recent accretions, and tried to get back to the original spirit of Muhammad, just like Luther and Calvin."

Let us, for a moment, indulge her assertion that Islam has gone through small reformations. Stop and ask, "What has been the result?" If the outcome of all these wonderful reformations has been Salafism and Islamic terror, then these small reformations do not mean that radical reform is no longer necessary.

Generally speaking, the outcome of reformation in Christianity resulted in a religious system that respects the basic values of human rights. Most churches do not promote killing people for converting, or beating women to discipline them, or stoning them to death for having extramarital sexual relations. In contrast, the outcome of what she calls "reformation" in Islam is a system that kills apostates, allows beating women, and justifies stoning them to death for sexual immorality. If the latter system does not need reformation then what does? Armstrong's assertions could be correct only if the majority of Muslims were followers of true Sufi Islam. But the reality is that most Islamic educational institutions and mosques promote Salafi Islam, which, without question, needs significant reformation.

One gets the sense that Armstrong conceives of Islam almost entirely in terms of the Quran. In the PBS interview, the word "hadith" does not appear, but terrorists are "not ordinary Muslims… who hear the basically peaceful message of the Qur'an". The "bedrock message" of the "Qur'an" is equality and sharing of wealth, she asserts. With the exception of a few sects, Islam consists of far, far more than the "Qur'an". Salafists employ passages in the hadiths and the *fiqh* that are perverted and violent. Ironically, the sects that reject the hadiths and look only to the Quran are persecuted. I was once a member of such a group, known as the Quranics. One of our leaders, Dr. Ahmed Subhy Mansour, was expelled from Al-Azhar University for being a member. Another, Mahmoud

Muhammad Taha, was judicially murdered in Sudan for his unorthodox Quranic views. Judging Islam solely on the Quran – as she appears to do – is an uneducated, primitive, and superficial approach; many of the problems in Islam are based on non-Quranic sources, such as the Sunna and Sira.

Perhaps more frustrating than all of her other comments is Armstrong's characterization of terrorists.

> *These were odd Muslims, and if they can break a Muslim law like drinking, then they can break other laws, too, like the law against killing innocent people and committing acts of terror. Richard Reed, the British shoe bomber, was a convert to Islam, and his imam in South London said they had to exclude him from the mosque because he came in saying, "Find me a jihad." Here was somebody who joined up because he wanted a fight. Similarly, an Australian boy picked up in Afghanistan at the same time as John Walker Lindh – they were drifters. They went from one group to another and finally ended up in Islam. These are not ordinary Muslims who go regularly to the mosque, who hear the basically peaceful message of the Qur'an. These are people who are spoiling for a fight, who are angry, who are not living good Muslim lives in other respects and are not characteristic of the Muslim people as a whole.*

Here, Armstrong's conception and presentation of terrorists is rife with flaws. Armstrong fails to understand the concept of *taqiyya*, or deceiving the enemy. Merely because the 9/11 hijackers drank alcohol and went to strip clubs does not make them bad Muslims if they are doing so to mislead unsuspecting communities by masking their true intentions. Worse, Armstrong suffers from the logical fallacy that the exception proves the rule. So what if John Walker Lindh was a "drifter" – a poor, forlorn fellow it seems – when jihadists enjoy heavily funded training camps, have perpetrated terror around the globe, and rely on an extensive ideological "bedrock" rooted in Salafism? Are we supposed to generalize about jihadists from the singular example of Lindh, and are we to dismiss the pervasiveness of Salafism because an imam happened to exclude Richard Reed from his mosque? If terrorists are isolated outcasts, what explains the fact that

Ayman al Zawahiri is a doctor and that *Jamaa Islamiya* was successful in universities and medical schools?

She continues,

> *Someone was saying to me recently that nearly all our former enemies end up on the White House lawn. Nelson Mandela, who's now regarded as a saint, was a couple of decades ago touted by the American administration as a communist and a terrorist. Arafat has appeared on that lawn. Now, I'm not going so far to say, goodness me, that Bin Laden will be there – of course not.*

Here, it is not clear what Armstrong is trying to say. Did the fact that Chamberlain visited Hitler make the fuehrer a savory person? Because Israel and the US made a terrible mistake in reviving Arafat, does that in itself recommend we treat terrorists as negotiating partners? Even more disturbing is how Armstrong plays down Islamic terror – Nelson Mandela didn't behead journalists on videotape.

I fully agree with Armstrong's loud proclamations against bigotry. But it is not bigotry for Westerners to be deeply concerned about Islam as they encounter it today, nor is it bigotry to criticize Islamic teaching. Indeed, without doing so we cannot combat Islamism. In fact, criticism of Salafists is having a positive and demonstrable impact. Recently, Gilliam Gibbons was released from her Sudanese jail cell because of Western pressure. The Saudi royal family, under tremendous criticism, absolved the latest gang-rape victim of 200 lashes. By playing down Salafism and indulging in moral equivalence, Karen Armstrong has made the problem of Islamism worse. She makes reform more difficult and actually interferes with the outrage of Westerners that is starting to yield results, however small.

Efraim Karsh (Head of Mediterranean Studies at King's College, University of London) has written a scathing review of Armstrong's book, *Muhammad: A Prophet for Our Time*. He cites Armstrongs comments after 9/11:

Muslims have never nurtured dreams of world conquest…. They had no designs on Europe, for example, even though Europeans imagined that they did. Once Muslim rule had been established in Spain, it was recognized that the empire could not expand indefinitely.

This is nothing short of an absurd, rewriting of history. It is also self-contradictory. If Muslims never dreamed of world conquest, what were they doing in Spain, 3000 miles from the Mecca?

Writes Karsh,

[her book is a] thinly veiled hagiography, depicting the prophet as a quintessential man of peace, "whose aim was peace and practical compassion" and who "literally sweated with the effort to bring peace to war-torn Arabia"; an altruistic social reformer of modest political ambitions, whose life was "a tireless campaign against greed, injustice, and arrogance" and who founded "a religion and cultural tradition that was not based on the sword but whose name — 'Islam' — signified peace and reconciliation."[62]

Armstrong's characterization of Prophet Muhammad might be plausible if Islam were reformed, but this is not how Muslims have portrayed the Prophet in non-Quranic sources. On several occasions he is shown to have exterminated the Jewish Qurayzah tribe and taken their women as sexual slaves.

Armstrong claims:

[T]he Qurayzah were not killed on religious or racial ground…. Muhammad had no ideological quarrel with the Jewish people.

Here is another example of falsification of history. Her assertion actually contradicts the traditional Islamic history books. These make it abundantly clear that Umar Ibn Al-Khatab, the second Islamic Caliph, expelled all Jews from Arabia based on instructions from Muhammad to cleanse the Arabian peninsula of other religions. Notably, Umar was one

---

[62]Efraim Karsh, "The Perfect Surrender", *The New York Sun*, September 25, 2006, http://www.nysun.com/article/40266?page_no=1

of only ten Muslims promised entry into Paradise by Prophet Muhammad.

Armstrong continues:

> *Later in the Islamic empires, Jews would enjoy full religious liberty and anti-Semitism would not become a Muslim vice until the Arab/ Israeli conflict became acute in the mid-twentieth century.*

It is true, that at certain specific times, Jews enjoyed more freedom in Muslim lands than in Europe, but they were always second-class dhimmis, under the threat of pogroms and oppression at any moment. The notion that anti-Semitism was not a "Muslim vice until the Arab/Israeli conflict" is preposterous.

Depressingly, none of the criticism leveled at Karen Armstrong has prevented the US military from recommending her book. In 2005, the New York Times made public the following reading list that Lieutenant General John H. Vines mandated to commanders:

A Reading List for Assignment to Iraq

Lt. Gen. John R. Vines, who is to take over as the American ground commander in Iraq, assigned these books to his top staff members:

"Islam: A Short History" by Karen Armstrong

"Islam for Dummies" by Malcolm Clark

"What Everyone Needs to Know About Islam" by John L. Esposito

"Unholy War: Terror in the Name of Islam" by Mr. Esposito

"The Reckoning: Iraq and the Legacy of Saddam Hussein" by Sandra Mackey

"Dereliction of Duty: Lyndon Johnson, Robert McNamara, the Joint Chiefs of Staff, and the Lies That Led to Vietnam" by H. R. McMaster

"The Clash of Civilizations and the Remaking of World Order" by Samuel P. Huntington

"Among the Believers: An Islamic Journey" by V.S. Naipaul

Nowhere in this list do we find such luminaries as Bernard Lewis and Fouad Ajami. Vice President of JihadWatch, Hugh Fitzgerald, has called this reading list the "greatest intelligence failure in the Iraq war."

As we can see, the Left is contributing to the Islamist catastrophe by giving an intolerant ideology the chance to infiltrate the Western world under the banner of freedom of religion. They defend the rights of Islamic systems which in turn hate our liberal values. One might have expected the members of the "progressive" movement to be the first to stand against the Islamic teaching that promotes polygamy, beating women, stoning them until death, and murdering gays by hanging. Instead our feminists and gay rights activists have allowed this ideology to flourish in our society. Mosques, Islamic schools, and Islamic libraries were freely opened in the Western world with the full blessing and sometimes the support of progressives.

The liberal values of freedom and human rights that we enjoy today are not the outcome of peace talks and mutual give-and-take with barbaric leaders. In fact, they are the outcome of the use of devastating military power against tyrants. The free world could not have put a stop to Hitler or the Japanese imperialist ambitions with negotiations and interfaith dialogue. It was the humiliating military defeat of the Nazi Germany and Japan that made room for change in their educational systems and thus precipitated their transformation into peace-loving societies.

We must choose between liberalism and Islamism. They simply cannot exist together. If we permit Sharia law in any form we will be permitting the most anti-liberal system on earth to thrive. Some may argue that if we limited the freedom of Salafists we would be equally as intolerant. But the difference is vast. Our democratic societies today promote values that respect life and value humanity. Salafists promote values of slavery, inequality, and hatred of life.

The distinction between good and evil here does not require a rocket scientist. But progressives have extended the concept of tolerance to tolerating cultures of brutality, and have not extended tolerance to anti-Islamist voices on our campuses. In doing so, our progressives have failed to learn a very important lesson from the immune system. Our immune system shows tolerance to the healthy cells in order to make the human body survive. However, the same 'tolerant' immune system does not show tolerance to cancer cells. In fact, the immune system destroys the new cancer cells that develop in our body. If the immune system did not make this distinction we would all develop cancer.

What world would we have today if our ancestors decided to show tolerance to slavery? Did the debates – or interfaith dialogue – between Jews and the leaders of the Spanish inquisition do any good? Was Nazism stamped-out with understanding? Most of us would acknowledge that tolerating such barbaric systems would have been a mistake. The same now applies to Islamism.

It would certainly be desirable to reform Islam and bring about a true, peaceful understanding of its texts. But that end has been frustrated, time and again, by Progressives who make excuses for Islamists. Claiming that Islam is peaceful without providing official interpretations that stand clearly against the violent edicts of Sharia law is very misleading and dangerous. As long as Salafists have Progressives to make excuses for them, many Muslims will continue to reject human rights and modernity.

Certainly, Islamic writings could be understood in a manner that encourages peace and tolerance. However, it is untrue to claim that the current way of teaching Islam promotes these values. A theologically rigorous re-interpretation of Islamic texts is necessary to bring about reformation. Insisting that there is nothing violent in today's mainstream Islamic teaching will only create more obstacles to reform. If Westerners think Islam, as it is taught today, is fine, what incentive is there for Muslims to reform their faith?

It is counterintuitive that that those typically branded as "conservative" have been at the forefront of the war against Islamism and those branded as "progressive" have enabled Islamic terror. We must unite to protect ourselves, our freedoms, and the next generation of Muslims from the devastating effects of Salafism.

Moral Relativism

A central obstacle in the West's battle with jihadism is the problem of moral relativism. By this we mean that the various failings of different cultures or religions are placed on an equal footing – they are assigned equal portions of blame. Moral relativism shows up in many places, for example, the repeated "cycle of violence" metaphor that the media applies to the Arab/Israeli conflict. For our purposes, however, we will examine the moral relativism that is applied to fundamentalist strains of Judaism and Christianity in juxtaposition to Salafism. I call this "Relative Fundamentalism".

Today, a Jewish fundamentalist is an observant Jew who strictly follows religious laws. A Christian fundamentalist is one who understands the Bible literally and might express anger or demonstrate against people who violate biblical commands (e.g., abortion, gay marriage). Except in a small number of isolated cases, these fundamentalists do not practice or accept violence, and especially, they refrain from murdering religious opponents. Furthermore, while Christians in the past have been violent in the name of their faith, the New Testament does not advocate violent behavior.

In contrast, a Muslim fundamentalist takes pleasure in burning a church or killing non-Muslims. He will applaud such acts if he doesn't commit them, ascribing them to the glory and power of Islam. Any rigorous statistical study will bear out that fundamentalist Muslims are responsible, per capita, for vastly higher rates of violence in comparison to fundamentalists of other faiths. Although, Muslims comprise a "mere" 20 percent of the world population, the number of violent acts perpetrated by them exceeds by far the number perpetrated in the name of other religions. Therefore, the word "Fundamentalism" must be redefined.

Moral relativists will argue that calls for violence appear in the Bible as well. Yet there is a vast difference. Biblical texts enjoin combat against specific groups of people in a particular territory at a precise time in history, often in response to misdeeds or unprovoked military attacks. Traditional Salafi Islamic texts, on the other hand, promote fighting and murdering people at all times, everywhere, solely based on their beliefs. In other words, Biblical violence took place in the past for particular motives; Islamic violence takes place today from a still-thriving universal injunction; that violence will remain with us until Islamic texts are reinterpreted.

For example, there is a huge chasm between wars of retribution against the ancient Amalek tribe and Salafist tenets that enjoin violence now and in the future. According to non-Quranic sources of Salafi Islam, Prophet Muhammad said,

> *I have been ordered by Allah to fight and kill all people (non-Muslims) until they say, "No God except Allah.*
> Sahih by Al-Buchary and Muslim

This hadith explains why Dr. Ayman Al-Zawahiri declared on videotape that violence against Americans will cease only when they submit to Islam.

The Amalek case is merely a historical event that happened against a specific nation, but the hadiths of Al-Buchary enjoin war on all infidels, for all time, if they do not submit to Islam. That is a critical distinction. Furthermore, the current teaching in both Judaism and Christianity does not allow violence against others while the current Salafi Islamic teaching promotes many violent values, including the one mentioned above; a review of current Islamic Sharia and jurisprudence books clearly show this to be the case.

If the danger of a religion's fundamentalism is defined by the number of terrorists it produces, then Islamism should be considered by far the most threatening form of it. Equating fundamentalism among different religions is misleading in this case because it ignores the magnitude of the problem. On the other hand, if fundamentalism is defined by the acceptance of violent precepts such as killing converts or using violence against women, then Islamism should also be considered a much bigger threat – many so-called "moderate" Muslims accept the violent edicts of Sharia. In this situation, a "moderate" Muslim could be more dangerous than a fundamentalist Jew or Christian. Thus, fundamentalism should be defined chiefly by an individual's violent beliefs, not by how he dresses or practices rituals.

For example, none of the orthodox Rabbis or devout Christians I know promotes or accepts the stoning of women to death for sexual immorality. On the other hand, many – if not most – of those who are considered moderate Muslims tacitly accepted this barbaric concept. Who should be described as a fundamentalist in this case? The silence of the Muslim world against stoning women to death in Saudi Arabia, Iran, and other Sharia-governed areas is clear evidence that there is a widespread problem in the Islamic world that needs special attention.

The proliferation of fundamentalist Islam in Muslim societies has resulted in uncivilized acts throughout the world and is responsible for grievous friction between societies. Clearly, to equate Islamic fundamentalism (Salafism) to Christian or Jewish fundamentalism is inaccurate. Yet it is precisely the inability of multiculturalists to comprehend *scale* that makes them dangerous. Has an abortion doctor been murdered by a Christian? Yes. Did Baruch Goldstein attack a mosque full of innocent worshippers? Yes. While these acts are deplorable, how do they compare to the 3000 murdered on 9/11, or to the barbaric terror attacks conducted by Islamists around the globe on a near-daily basis?

Progressives object to restrictions placed on Salafist incitement under the banner of freedom of speech. They claim that it is impossible to determine which speech should be restricted and which should be permitted. This dilemma, however, can be resolved in terms of physical consequences of the incitement versus psychological consequences. One of the main problems we find in Progressives is their inability to find clear borders for the word "wrong". This stems from their perception that immorality is a relative issue. But any reasonable individual can place a dividing line between thoughts that do not cause harm to others and thoughts that promote direct physical harm. For example, it does no physical harm when someone rejects the existence of a God, but when a person believes, or teaches his children to believe that non-believers must convert, or pay the *jizya*, or be killed, it leads to physical harm. Thus, whenever speech advocates *physical* harm, it should be restricted.

Chapter 5:

Toward Islamic Reformation

Chapter 5: Toward Islamic Reformation

Obstacles to Reformation

Salafist Resistance

The Salafists have established a system that suppresses any attempt to meaningfully reform Islam. Those who would change the teachings are threatened with hellfire (as we have noted earlier). Those who actually alter Salafist teachings are declared Infidels (*Kafereen*); they are not only destined for Hell but are eligible for destruction in this life. Salafists threaten Reformers with Redda Law – a component of Shariia which justifies killing Muslims who convert or depart from accepted doctrine (*Maaloom Mina Al-deen Bildarura*). Examples of Islamic reformers who were murdered based on Redda Law include Dr. Farag Fouda in Egypt (killed June 8, 1992 after a *fatwa* of apostasy was issued against him); Dr. Rashad Khalifa in the US (stabbed to death, January 31, 1990 at his Tucson, Arizona mosque); and Muhammad Taha in 1985 in Sudan.

Salafists also teach that violent Islamic texts are fundamental to the religion. Muslims therefore worry that Islam might disintegrate if reformed; they learn to see the religion as a house of cards that can collapse if touched. Thus, resistance to reformation becomes instinctual. Reformers and their families are almost guaranteed to be boycotted or threatened by the local Muslim community. Finally, Salafists have waged unceasing doctrinal warfare on Sufi and Secular Muslims. For example, when Sufis visit shrines to ask for blessings, Salafists proclaim them infidels and idolaters, based on the following verse:

> ...*whereas those whom you invoke instead of Him do not own so much as the husk of a date-stone! If you invoke them, they do not hear your call; and even if they could hear, they would not (be able to) respond to you. And (withal,) on the Day of Resurrection they will utterly disown your having associated them with God. And none can make thee understand [the truth] like the One who is all-aware.*
> {Quran 35:13- 14}

Secular Muslims are branded as infidels as well:

> ....*those who do not judge with Allah's law are Infidels (or Idolaters).*
> {Quran 5:44}

The use of these representative verses by Salafists has deterred many young Muslims from following Sufi or Secular paths. Many Muslims have therefore come to believe that Salafi teachings are the only accepted version of Islam. This unmitigated intimidation has paralyzed the thinking process in the Islamic population; Muslims are afraid to challenge Salafism and its violent injunctions.

Information, Transmission, Perception

In the abstract, we can usefully conceptualize the obstacles to reformation on three levels: information, transmission, and perception. When we say "information", we mean the ideas and interpretations that are specifically being conveyed. In other words, it is the "ammunition", or doctrine of reformation with which Muslims are armed to make them resistant to violence. Reformation is obstructed at the information level when it lacks a rigorous theological foundation for true peace and tolerance. Our job, then, on the information level, is to construct that rigorous foundation.

When we speak of "transmission", we mean the mechanism by which ideas of reformation are conveyed. Even if a reformer possessed a rigorously peaceful interpretation of Islam, he would need to transmit that doctrine in order to educate other Muslims. Obstacles to transmission include physical threats from Salafists and the lack of a dedicated medium of communication – for example, a television channel or a publishing company willing to risk capital on the project.

Finally, by "perception" we mean the way in which a doctrine of reformation is perceived by the Muslim community. A reformer could have a rigorous doctrine of reform, he could have a well-functioning mechanism of transmission, but he will still face negative perceptions of his new interpretations.

Many Muslim communities believe any new approach which contradicts the traditional teachings will cause the religion to disintegrate. But if they assist the disintegration of Islam, Muslims would face eternal damnation. So to avoid hellfire, they reject the new doctrine. One can use the finest technological tools to transmit information, but it will fail to produce an effect if the receiver's radio is not operating. Merely because a television channel exists does not mean viewers are watching that channel. An example of just such a problem became apparent when the US government funded programs to win the "heart and minds" of Muslims (e.g. *Al-Hura* Channel and *Hi* Magazine). Those programs were not successful. Information was made available, but perceptual resistance insured that these initiatives did not have the desired effect.

In order to bring about a reformation of Islam, all three levels of resistance will need to be addressed. On the other hand, if any one of these levels is not addressed, any attempt at reformation will fail.

Inadequate Criteria for Virtue

One obstacle to reform that operates on the perception level is worth singling out for comment: the commonly understood criteria for being a "good Muslim" are based on empty ritual rather than on firm, moral justification.

It is widely believed that a Muslim who fulfils the Five Pillars of Islam is virtuous. These pillars are 1) accept no God but Allah and Muhammad as his prophet, 2) pray five times per day, 3) fast on Ramadan, 4) give alms, and 5) perform the *haj* (Pilgrimage). Unfortunately, these pillars are mainly rituals.

As a result, Muslims may see jihadists behead someone on videotape and still perceive them to be good Muslims because they follow the Five Pillars. This inadequate test for goodness explains, in part, why so many Muslims fail to criticize or demonstrate against Islamism and Islamic Terror. Deep in their mind they feel that Islamic terrorists cannot be bad Muslims because they perform these superficial rituals. It is one reason why we do not see truly serious *fatawa* against terrorists by Islamic scholars.

If the moral structure of a Muslim's worldview were built on humane values, rather than on five rituals, it would help pave the way to a more peaceful Islam. In itself, obsession with the "Five Pillars" is strange because the concept of "Five Pillars" is never mentioned anywhere in the Quran (it is only mentioned in the hadiths). On the other hand, injunctions to virtuous, moral behavior are available in the holy book. Unfortunately, for whatever reasons, these positive injunctions are not by themselves considered a main foundation of the religion.

Lack of a Peaceful Theological Foundation

Inexact Non-Violence

Both Sufi and Secular Islam are weak in their theological foundation. When Sufi or secular Muslims are challenged as to why they have preferred a non-violent action, or why they recommend a peaceful path, they do not have recourse to the same doctrinal bedrock in Islam that Salafists enjoy.

The Sufi belief system relies on an individual's spiritual condition rather than a literal understanding of Islamic writings. Sufis believe that the word of God does not need an interpreter and that the believer does not require an explanation of Quranic verses. Each believer must endeavor to understand the religion via a personal, subjective experience with God. Consequently, Sufi masters did not preoccupy themselves with writing explanations (tafseer) for the Quran which convey peaceful understanding.

Therefore, while the Sufi belief system may be attractive to many, it suffers from the defect of theological imprecision. The result is that Sufi and Secular Muslims find it difficult to resists their Salafist counterparts. For example, a young Muslim is confused by the following Quranic verse

> ...*slay the Idolaters (Infidels) wherever you may come upon them...*
> {Quran 9:5}

He asks three different Islamic scholars – Sufi, Secular and Salafi– to interpret it. The Sufi scholar might offer, "Love everybody and be kind to all people". The young Muslim finds this unsatisfying and insists that the verse explicitly enjoins him to kill infidels everywhere. The Sufi cleric tries again, "You will understand the significance of the verse in the Day of Judgment – Allah wants you to love everyone". Dissatisfied, the young Muslim approaches a secular Muslim, who responds, "I'm not sure, my understanding of Islam is that it is a "religion of peace". Finally, a Salafist is approached. He utilizes ample material from authorized Islamic textbooks which justifies violence against non-Muslims.

Since the Sufi and secular Muslims lack a powerful theological base, the young Muslim more often than not is attracted to Salafi Islam. After all, the Salafist can "back up" his claims.

Rigorous Hatred

Because the hatred and violence espoused by the Salafist has a strong supporting body of doctrine, his version has become mainstream. Salafism is the default doctrine in most (if not all) Islamic schools, mosques, and universities.

As we mentioned at the start, Islam is comprised, from a doctrinal perspective, of several components. These are: the Quran (word of Allah), the *Hadith* and *Sunna* (words and deeds of Prophet Muhammad), the exploits of the *Sahaba*

(Disciples of the Prophet), the Islamic jurisprudence schools (*fiqh*), and the tafseer or commentaries on the Quran. One might expect, therefore, that should a verse in the Quran enjoin violence, other components of the religion would counterbalance it with a peaceful interpretation or limit the scope of the verse to its period of history. The sad reality is that non-Quranic components do not properly offset violent verses and, in fact, supplement their violent nature.

For example, the following verse in the Quran…

> *Fight those who believe not in Allah nor the Last Day, nor hold that forbidden which hath been forbidden by Allah and His Messenger (Muhammad), nor acknowledge the religion of Truth (Islam), [even if they are] of the People of the Book (Christians and Jews), until they pay the Jizya (Humiliation Tax) with submission, and feel themselves subdued.*
>   {Quran 9: 29}

…is supported by a Hadith:

> *Narrated Ibn Omar, Prophet Muhammad said, "I have been ordered by Allah to fight and kill all people (non-Muslims) until they say, "No God except Allah". (Sahih by Al-Buchary and Muslim)*

It is also supported by the Sahaba. One such disciple was Umar Ibn Al-Khatab. He declared many wars against Jews and Christians in order to subjugate them to Islam. The reader will recall Caliph Umar's official decree:

> *Christians shall not build, in cities or in their neighborhood, new monasteries, Churches, convents, or monks' cells, nor shall they repair, by day or by night, such of them as fall in ruins or are situated in the quarters of the Muslims.*
>
> *[Etc…]*

This declaration is considered legitimate and valid by most – if not all – Islamic authorities today.

The problem is not only that various Hadiths and *Sahaba* support violent verses in the Quran, but that the *tafseer* or commentaries invalidate peaceful verses. This technique is called "abrogation". It relies on the fact that Prophet Muhammad (as mentioned in many Islamic books) revealed verses at different times, and that the peaceful verses were revealed in the earlier Mecca period, when Muhammad lacked the strength to declare war. Later, in Medina, Muhammad had the strength to do so and revealed verses that were violent. Salafists use the chronology to insist that later, violent verses cancel the earlier, peaceful ones.

In Arabic, "abrogated" is known as *mansuch*. I will never forget when I presented a peaceful verse of the Quran to my Salafi friend Adel Seif. I had viewed him as a mentor, but when I showed him a verse that permitted Muslims to stop hating Jews and Christians, his immediate comment was that my verse is abrogated by the "Sword verse" {Quran 9:5}. His response was not, strictly speaking, his own; it is the traditional view of Salafists in general.

It is this abrogation that allows Salafists to deceive non-Muslims into believing that Islam is a "religion of peace". To non-Muslims, Salafists present the peaceful verses. To their own flock, they present the violent verses and teach that they abrogate the peaceful ones. Therefore, Islam could be the "religion of peace" only if Muslim scholars provided a theologically-rigorous doctrine that stands unambiguously against the violence and hate. Until such Islamic scholars do so, the problem of violent Islam will remain with us.

How to Reform Islam

How then, do we reform Islam? To answer this question, I will briefly outline what a program of Islamic reformation should look like. What we need are a "toolbox" and a "roadmap" – a collection of strategies and tactics for implementing reform in conjunction with a series of steps.

De-emphasize non-Quranic writings

We have seen that many violent tenets in Islam do not have their source in the Quran, but in secondary writings. These writings are not the word of God. The task of reforming Islam into a peaceful religion will therefore be eased if we rely on the Quran more and de-emphasize or even reject many non-Quranic texts.

For example, Redda Law dictates that apostates be killed. However, Redda Law is not rooted in the Quran. By eliminating Redda Law, scholars could reduce the theological justification for killing apostates. Similarly, common punishments in Islam, such as stoning women or killing homosexuals are never mentioned in the Quran. If we jettison or revise those Islamic texts that advocate these punishments, Islam will become more humane.

Special attention should be paid to a re-examination of the Hadiths. As the reader may remember, the *Sunna* were written down in the hadiths long after the death of Muhammad and are therefore classified into different official levels of accuracy. These classifications were determined by scholars centuries ago, so the hadiths should be reevaluated for accuracy. A new level of accuracy needs to be introduced: "Guaranteed Hadiths". These guaranteed versions must be hadiths that show the peaceful, virtuous words and deeds of Muhammad. It must be remembered that the Hadiths, like other non-Quranic writings, are not the word of Allah and can be filtered and packaged anew, just as the scholars of old did when they compiled them.

By itself, merely relying on the Quran is still not sufficient to make Islam peaceful. There are still violent passages in the Quran, and these require a different technique for interpretation because they are the word of God. We cannot simply cancel or jettison a *sura* or *ayat*. Abrogation is only permissible in the first place because peaceful verses chronologically precede the violent ones. However, revising and re-evaluating non-Quranic writings will establish a precedent of reform so that new ideas can penetrate the religion more easily. Today, reformers are suppressed; they fear for their lives every time they offer an interpretation that departs from traditional tenets, because in doing so they risk being labeled apostates.

Importance of "The" (Al-)

In addition to re-examining non-Quranic writings, it is important to return to the violent passages in the Quran to see what can be done. There is a technique to limit the violent verses that does not cancel or abrogate them – we can limit their scope to the historical time period when they were revealed. This can be done rigorously – it is not a subjective notion. The key to this rigor are the simple Arabic letters "Al-", or "the". While this may seem like a legalistic or formalistic sleight of hand, it is perfectly legitimate and profoundly important.

The word "the" is a definite article that refers to something specific. When "the" is absent, the object of a statement is universal; when it is present, it refers to a specific subset of a collection. We can interpret the definite article "Al" to mean specifically those targets that existed in Prophet Muhammad's time period and location.

For example, *mn kafar* means "infidels" in the universal sense, whereas *al-kafreen* means "the infidels", the specific infidels referred to at the time. Thus, there is a big difference between killing *mn kafar* and killing *al-kafreen*. It happens that the Quran never employs the article *mn* in reference to wars against non-believers but almost always employs *al-*.

Consider the following verse:

> ...*slay the Infidels wherever you may come upon them*...
> {Qur'an 9:5}

A Muslim who interprets the verse without considering the definite article "the" may join a jihadist organization. On the other hand, if he paid attention to the word "the", he would be perfectly justified to regard the statement strictly in its historical context. We have seen how, as a former jihadist, these verses played a key role in my indoctrination process. Had I learned to consider the prefix "the", it would have dramatically weakened the injunctions to brutality.

The following are some examples of the Quranic verses that jihadists employ to incite violence. As the reader will notice, all of them use "the":

> *The infidels are your sworn enemies* {Quran 4:101}

> *Make war on the infidels who dwell around you* {Quran 9:123}

> *When you meet the Infidels in the battlefield, strike off their heads* {Quran 47:4}

> *Mohamed is Allah's apostle. Those who follow him are ruthless to the infidels* {Quran 48:29}

> *Prophet, make war on the infidels* {Quran 66:9}

> *Never be a helper to the disbelievers* {Quran 28:86}

> *Kill the disbelievers wherever we find them* {Quran 2:191}

> *Therefore, when you meet the infidels (unbelievers), smite their necks until you overcome them fully, and then tighten their bonds; but thereafter [set them free,] either by an act of grace or against ransom, so that the burden of war may be lifted.*
>   {Quran 47:4}

It is amazing that this vital emphasis on the word "the" – an emphasis that can mean the difference between life and death – is not available in any approved *tafseer* of the Quran. I believe that if Islamic terrorist leaders like Dr. Al-Zawahiri or Bin Laden would have been taught the Quran with this emphasis, they may not have declared war on non-Muslims, and perhaps Islamic terrorism would not exist.

Two letters can make a considerable difference.

Relativity of the Quran

In the Quran there are verses that Salafists utilize to justify abrogation. Reinterpreting these abrogation verses eases the transition to a non-violent Islam. This will allow young Muslims to see the whole religion in the shadow of the peaceful verses instead of the reverse.

Muslims are permitted by Allah himself to follow the verses that better suit their point in history and disregard others which do not. When modern laws and Islamic law conflict, as is the case with severe physical punishment, Muslims can apply modern judgments about human rights to resolve the impasse. The Quran permits Muslims to exercise discretion so as to follow more peaceful verses.

> *And follow the better of (the Quranic verses) revealed to you from your Lord.*
> {Quran 39:55}

We might call this preference for certain verses over others the "Relativity of the Quran". It provides essential flexibility to Muslims who must practice a peaceful version of the religion, one that lives in harmony with other faiths in various societies.

The Relativity of the Quran encourages Muslims to think at the concept level rather than at the literal level. For example, a literal understanding of the Quran permits a Muslim to marry more than one wife. At the concept level, the Muslim will know that polygamy applied in the early stages of Islam and that the Quran forbids being unjust to others. Conceptual thinking is therefore helpful in promoting values of decency.

Promote the Humane Side of Prophet Muhammad

When I became a more dedicated Muslim my dream was to emulate Prophet Muhammad in all his actions. Muslims are encouraged to do so by the following Quranic verse:

> *Ye have indeed in the Messenger of Allah a beautiful pattern (of conduct) for any one whose hope is in Allah and the Final Day, and who engages much in the Praise of Allah.*
> {Quran 33:21}

In fact, following in the footsteps of Prophet Muhammad is the ultimate target of most – if not all – devout Muslim men.

Muhammad can be a positive role model. Many of his traits, as described in numerous verses of Quran, are worthy of emulation. For example, Muhammad was instructed to assist his enemy during war if the latter became helpless:

> *If one amongst the Pagans (during the war) ask thee for asylum, grant it to him and give your hand of help to him, so that he may hear the word of God and then assist him to reach where he can feel secure and safe.*
> {Quran 9:6}

Other positive aspects include:

> *But forgive them [the Infidels], and say "Peace! (on you)" But soon shall they know!*
> {Quran 43:89}

> *If then they refused to follow you, we have not sent you as a guard over them. Your duty is (only) but to convey (the Message).*
> Quran {42:48}

> *If they accuse you of falsehood, say: "Your Lord is full of mercy all-embracing; but from people in guilt never will His wrath be turned back.*
> {Quran 6:147}

> *Say, "The truth (Islam) is from your God": it is up to any person to follow it or not. "*
> {Quran 18:29}

Imitating these injunctions and patterns can, in most circumstances, produce a virtuous and peaceful outcome.

However, in Salafi books, the following Quranic verse is understood to mean that Muhammad was allowed certain privileges above all other Muslims:

> *The Prophet has a higher claim on the believers than (they have on) their own selves, (seeing that he is as a father to them) and his wives are their mothers (i.e. not allowed to marry any other person).*
> {Quran 33:6}

Taking this Quranic verse as a cue, the description of Prophet in the Sunna and Hadith books show a much different side of Muhammad. We have mentioned some of these in the first chapter, but here are more. According to the classical theologian al-Qurtubi, these privileges include:

> *if (Prophet Muhammad) looked at a woman her husband has to divorce her and Muhammad is allowed to marry her to have sex ... if he divorced a woman it is not allowed for anyone to marry her ... and he was allowed to take for himself the food from the hungry and the water from the thirsty....*
> Tafseer al-Qurtubi, Surat al-Ahzab

> *The Prophet married her (Aisha) when she was six years old and he consummated his marriage when she was nine years old, and then she remained with him for nine years.*
> Sahih al-Buchary

> *According to Aisha, "The Prophet engaged me when I was a girl of six (years). We went to Medina and stayed at the home of Bani-al-Harith bin Khazraj. Then I got ill and my hair fell down. Later on my hair grew (again) and my mother, Um Ruman, came to me while I was playing in a swing with some of my girl friends. She called me, and I went to her, not knowing what she wanted to do to me. She caught me by the hand and made me stand at the door of the house. I was breathless then, and when my breathing became all right, she took some water and rubbed my face and head with it. Then she took me into the house. There in the house I saw some Ansari women who said, "Best wishes and Allah's Blessing and good luck." Then she gave me to them and they prepared me (for the marriage). Unexpectedly*

Allah's Apostle came to me in the forenoon and my mother handed me over to him, and at that time I was a girl of nine years of age.
  Sahih al-Buchary

The reader is free to imagine the impact such hadith verses can have on a dedicated Muslim who insists on emulating Muhammad.

The relationship of Muslims to Muhammad and their love to him is extraordinary. This was exemplified in the violent demonstrations of hundreds of thousands of Muslims in response to the Muhammad Cartoons. Their love and obedience to the prophet has reached such a fever that a highly-educated professor like Dr. Aisha Abdul-Rahman (Bint Alshateii) praised Muhammad's marriage to a 7-year-old girl when the Prophet was fifty. Here is a passage is from her famous book *Nessa Allnabi* which means, "The Women of the Prophet Muhammad":

> *And He Muhammad, Allah praise him, knew Aisha since she was in her very early childhood and he put her in the position of his dear daughter. He observed her growth and her sexual development that created attractive beauty…. and it is written in the most accurate books for the Hadith Al-Buchary and Muslim, that Muhammad used to say to Aisha when she was a child, 'I have seen you twice in my dreams as some one was covered by a white dress made out of silver and I heard a voice saying to me this is your wife. When I removed the silver cover I found you, then the voice, a revelation, said to me this is your wife…. so I said since this is the will of Allah, let it happen.*

The conversation referred to between Prophet Muhammad and Aisha is supposed to have happened before Aisha was seven. The Cultural Mind of Dr. Abdul-Rahman would certainly reject the idea of marrying a man of fifty-two to a girl of seven, however, the professor's extreme love of the Prophet and fear of critiquing him – and the eternal damnation she would receive if she did – combine to create a Religious Mind that suppresses her conscience.

The dilemma created by Muhammad would be much less burdensome if the Prophet was approached in his historical and cultural context. But that is not the case. In contrast, among Jews King David is widely criticized for his adultery and treatment of Uriah. Yet while it is easy to find many Christians and Jews who are critical of King David, it is virtually impossible to find a devout Muslim who is willing to criticize any action of Muhammad. The result is a professor who inexorably finds herself advocating pedophilia[63] – something we hope will not be tolerated in the West under the banner of religious freedom.

The esteem for the Prophet that many Muslims feel is, in many situations, more prominent than their attachment to Allah himself. As many may have observed, the reaction to the Muhammad Cartoons was much more global and violent than reactions to Quran desecration. This love for Muhammad could be partially due to the concept of *Al-Shaffaa*, or "intercession". That is, when some Muslims go to Hell by the order of Allah (on judgment day), the Prophet may intercede with Allah on behalf of the sinner so that the sinner may enter Paradise. Therefore, in the subconscious of many Muslims, Allah has in fact become an oppressor figure while Muhammad has become their savior. This conflation of roles has created a form of devotion to the Prophet that can actually exceed the love Muslims have for Allah. This type of love for Muhammad is probably the reason why Muslims praise him with PBUH ("peace be upon him") whenever his name is mentioned – and critically, fail (in most cases) to use the same phrase in conjunction with "Allah". The Quran technically recommends[64] that Muslims use praise in both cases – with Muhammad and Allah. This "selective" praising speaks volumes.

If Muslims followed mainly the Quranic verses instead of the hadiths, many of the problems related to emulation of Prophet Muhammad could be solved. Most (but not all) of

---

[63]That Prophet Muhammad married a girl of seven is not mentioned in the Quran itself – it is mentioned in the Hadiths.

[64]{Quran 87:1} Praise the name of your Lord (God) *and* {Quran 33:56} Send your blessings on him (Mohamed).

the negative examples of Muhammad's conduct are not in the Quran, but in books written much later. Islamic sects that reject the Hadiths are far less conflicted and tortured because they reject most of the stories about him not found in the Quran. Doing so has enabled these sects to emphasize the positive aspects of Muhammad's conduct. Alternatively, it is not necessary to reject all of the Hadiths – we are free to reclassify violent Hadiths as inaccurate and offer a new category of hadiths – "Guaranteed" – for hadiths that are peaceful.

Accept Jews and Judaism

Many Muslim scholars and clergy promote the notion that Jews are apes and pigs, and that Muslims must kill every Jew before the end of days. These hateful proclamations are a serious barrier to genuine peace between Arabs and Israel. It is unlikely that any Arab child who has been brainwashed with this Jew-hatred will be able to live in harmony with Jews in the future.

Clerics attempt to justify Jew-hatred by employing passages in the Quran and in the Hadiths:

> *Shall I point out to you something much worse than this by the treatment it received from Allah those who incurred the curse of Allah and His wrath (the Jews), those of whom some He transformed into monkeys and pigs (the Jews),, those who worshipped evil - these are (many times) worse in rank, and far more astray from the even path!*
> {Quran 5:60}

> *The Hour will not come until the Muslims fight the Jews (and the Muslims will kill them), until the Jews hide behind the trees and rocks and the trees and rocks will say, "O Muslim, 0 Servant of God, Here are the Jews, Come and kill them!"*
> Sahih Al-Buchary

How do we approach these two representative passages? The second citation is a hadith, and as we have mentioned, it is not the Quran and therefore is not the literal word of God. We are justified in calling it inaccurate since it was compiled and set down by some Islamic scholars more than two hundred years after the death of the Prophet. As to the first citation, it is from the Quran – but notice that the phrase "the Jews" is in parentheses; the word "Jew" or "Jews" is not actually in the Quran. These words were added by later interpreters. Therefore, we can combat these violent interpretations by eliminating the insertion of "Jews" that we see. In other words, "the Jews" is part of a *tafseer*, or commentary on the Quran and is not sacred. When we examine the verse without the hateful *tafseer*, we see that it can yield an entirely different meaning – one that does not promote Jew-hatred.

Indeed, Islamic scholars have intensified the hatred of Jews by adding words in brackets to explicitly limit instances where the "Children of Israel" are praised. The Saudis make freely available – to mosques around the world – translations of the Quran with these limiting *tafseer*. Here is one such example, where the clerics added a parenthesized comment:

> *Children of Israel! Call to mind the favor which I bestowed upon you, and that I preferred you to all other nations (of your time period, in the past)*
> {Quran 2:47}

The actual verse is this:

> *Children of Israel! Call to mind the favor which I bestowed upon you, and that I preferred you to all other nations.*
> {Quran 2:47}

These changes distort the positive references to Jews in the Quran, and the have become common to most approved translations and commentary.

It is incredibly hypocritical that Muslim scholars added the word ("Jews") to the verse related to "pigs and monkeys", while they added the phrase "of your time period, in the past" to limit praise for the "children of Israel". If it is acceptable to historicize the verses, then surely we can do so with "the"; and if it is acceptable to add commentary, then surely we can add our own or remove existing commentary.

This typical Salafi approach to Islamic writings has amplified Jew-hatred in our time to an unprecedented level. Muslims must seek a new, peaceful relationship with the Jewish people. Most prophets who are mentioned in the Quran are Jews, so it is unacceptable –according to the Quran – to attack the Jews of today based on the conflicts Muhammad had with them in the 7th century. As Quran 17:15 tells us, no bearer of burdens can bear the burden of another. This is similar to the biblical injunction not to blame the son for the sins of the father.

Justify Good Values Rigorously

Salafi Scholars teach that religious freedom, gender equality, and Gay rights are not Islamic. Islam as it is taught today promotes killing those who leave the religion; permits beating women and polygamy, and permits murdering gays. When I was a member of *Jamaa Islamiya* with Dr. Al-Zawahiri, we hated the West mainly because of its freedom and civil liberties. We believed that they violated fundamental tenets of Sharia law.

Looking at the Quran from a different but rigorous angle can make Quranic teachings compatible with human rights and provide the doctrinal justification for modern values that Muslims require.

The Quran stated clearly:

> *Hold to forgiveness; and command Muslims to follow the "Urf" - which is commonly accepted among mankind.*
> {Quran 2:47}

According to this verse, Muslims are instructed to follow what is commonly acceptable among enlightened people. This verse could be applied to accommodate civil rights and laws of secular societies.

Some Muslims feel uncomfortable applying one verse while ignoring another, or rejecting a given Islamic text. However, the "Relativity of the Quran" gives us the justification we need, based on the following verses:

And follow the 'better' of what is revealed to you from your Lord...
{Quran 2:47}

Say the good news to those who worship me. Those who listen to the Word, and follow the best meaning (Wherever it is found): those are the ones whom G-d has guided, and those are the ones endowed with understanding.
{Quran 39:17-18}

These verses permit Muslims to prefer using certain verses because they are the "best meaning" or the "better of what is revealed" for a given stage of human civilization. They also permit Muslims to learn from other cultures and live at peace with them, minimizing the "clash of civilizations".

Speaking the truth, even if it hurts, is essential. It may involve painful critiques of Muslim actions in Islamic history, such as the Islamic Conquest. In this case, Muslims will require the rigorous justification provided by the following verse:

O ye who believe! Stand out firmly for justice, as witnesses to G-d, even as against yourselves, or your parents, or your kin.
{Quran 4:135}

This verse clearly permits the self-criticism that is a prerequisite for tolerance.

As we have noted many times, it is essential to promote the value of critical thinking in the Islamic curriculum. Once again, the Quran supports this effort, for example:

Behold, verily in these things there are signs for those who think!
{Quran 13:4}

Believing that non-believers will go to Hell causes Muslims to hate non-Muslim societies and paves the way toward terrorism. But the Quran commands Muslims not to be judgmental:

> *Then it will be for Us (only God) to call them to account.*
> {Quran 88:25}

Thus, it is important to promote values of humanity and virtue, and to do so rigorously. The Quran can be utilized effectively for this purpose – indeed, it must.

Chapter 6:

Strategic Plan to Defeat Radical Islam

Chapter 6: Strategic plan to defeat radical Islam

In our attempt to combat Islamism and Islamic terror we must realize that there is no single magical solution. Military power alone will not solve it; education alone won't either. It is only through the efficient combination and integration of different tactics that we can achieve victory in the War on Terror. But before we can fight Islamism we must understand what it is. To do so, we must analyze the problem objectively to identify the contributing factors.

The proliferation of violent Islam in Islamic societies has typically followed a standard pattern. The process starts with the propagation of Salafi ideology within a community. Increasing numbers of women begin to wear the *hijab*. The *hijab* is both a symptom of Salafi proliferation and a catalyst for Islamism – it helps spread the ideology itself. In turn, the proliferation of Salafism and the *hijab* lead to the mentality of passive terrorism. Passive terrorists, as we have mentioned, do not actually perpetrate terrorist attacks. However, they want to implement oppressive Sharia law and quietly lend support to active terrorists by failing to denounce them properly. Because they want to implement Sharia and do not respect secular rule, the growth in the numbers of passive terrorists is a real threat to any free society. A very small – but significant – fraction of the passive terrorists develops into a body of active terrorists. It follows that by decreasing the number of passive terrorists we decrease the number of active terrorists, and thus, decrease the number of terrorist attacks.

In addition, Islamists exploit anti-American and anti-Western propaganda to incite more hatred and fuel more Islamization. A careful observation of Islamic communities either in the Muslim world or in the West shows beyond doubt that the production of jihadists follows this pattern, illustrated in figure three. Once we understand the Islamization process we can begin conceiving of an effective strategy to defeat it.

The diagram shows us that we will not be effective if we strictly attempt to prevent terrorist attacks and ignore the entire process.

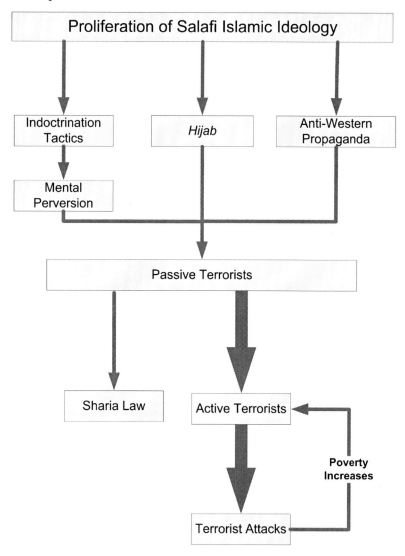

Figure 3 – the Islamic Terrorism Cycle

The first strategic step to combat Islamization is at the ideological level. A new interpretation of Islamic texts is needed to counterbalance the violent interpretations of the Salafists. Simply omitting the violent passages from school curricula and replacing them with peaceful ones is insufficient. Muslim children will learn peaceful verses at school during the day and learn the violent passages at Mosques in the evening. As we have seen, Salafists utilize abrogation to cancel the peaceful passages in the Quran. A new rigorously-peaceful foundation for Islam will limit violent verses only to their historical context and thereby open the gate for the Quran to be understood in the light of peaceful ones.

Furthermore, educational systems need to be created which teach young Muslims peace. The curriculum should promote critical thinking and be structured in opposition to Salafist indoctrination. Peaceful education needs to begin at an earlier age, before jihadists have the chance to reach young minds. Proper cognitive psychology tactics should be utilized to prepare the curriculum and promote values of modernity and humanity. Encouraging peaceful sects in Islam such as 'true' Sufis or other genuinely peaceful groups will also help foster change at the ideological and educational levels.

In addition, improving the image of the US in the Islamic world will help disrupt the Islamization process and assist counter-terror efforts. However, a program to win "hearts and minds" must be carefully thought out and implemented in such a way as to prevent the loss of American dignity. Apologizing for a few military personnel, for example, will not do. Granting too many concessions is perceived as weakness and only aggravates the problem of Islamism. We have shown that US foreign policy is not the cause of Islamic terror. Negative images of the US operate at the perception level – any improvement of America's image will therefore not stem from drastic changes in policy. It is important not to fight yesterday's wars. Utilizing the same cold-war tactics that worked against the Soviets will not necessarily be helpful in winning the hearts and minds of Muslim nations. They are two different cultures and the approach that worked with the former may actually produce the opposite outcome in the latter.

It goes without saying that Western governments must pool information to weaken the financial support behind Salafi Islam and to disrupt the communication between Salafi propagandists. The integration of effective intelligence, ideological, and psychological tactics will impede the transformation of passive terrorists into active ones.[65] Synchronized efforts on these fronts will decrease the frequency of terrorism incidents.

The use of alternative energy must be supported. Governments must mandate more efficient petrol engines to reduce the addiction to foreign oil. This will weaken Wahabbi financial support for Salafi Islam.

Finally, there is little doubt that efficient use of military force is crucial to the overall success in the War on Terror. We must remember that the civilized world could not combat Nazism without defeating it first at the military level. We did not overcome Hitler by peace negotiations or mutual understanding; it was the devastating military power that ended his barbaric regime and cleared a path for peace and democracy. Indeed, World War II furnishes us with an excellent example of the dynamic relationship between military force and ideological transformation. Everyone hopes that tyrants would change their violent programs by dialogue; but the reality is that they have to first be defeated militarily. In other words, military intervention facilitates the whole process of educational reform.

Unfortunately, we can only conclude that the US has utilized insufficient military resolve. Firing cruise missiles at a few terrorist targets is like using half a dose of antibiotics to treat

[65]Tactical details of this strategy are beyond the scope of this book but the author is willing to explain them with appropriate bodies.

an infection. When we do so, the infection is not cured, but resistant strains of bacteria arise.

When the CIA had located bin Laden, Clinton balked at the use of force because he feared collateral civilian casualties. The outcome of that decision was that thousands of innocents died on 9/11. It is a sad fact that in many wars there is no easy moral escape. If we obsess about the humane treatment of our enemies, we jeopardize the lives of our own people. It is also true that terrorists use human shields to discourage attackers, or in the event of casualties, to win a propaganda victory. These tactics should not deter us from using force.

Nobody supports the intentional killing of innocent civilians. But in war, as in medicine, good "cells" sometimes die when we "treat" bad ones. If we wish to save the life of a cancer patient, we employ chemotherapy or radiation, and doing so kills non-cancerous cells in the process. In such a situation, it is unfair to blame the doctor for killing good cells, because doing so is inevitable if the patient is to be saved. As in cancer treatment, we must seek to minimize collateral damage, but we must also realize that it cannot be avoided. I will certainly support any approach that can stop terror without losing any human soul. But as long as jihadists employ human shields, we must resign ourselves to the collateral loss of innocent life. It is the responsibility of Islamic scholars to prevent collateral damage by denouncing the use of human shields.

Conclusion

Islamism comprises the lion's share of mainstream Islam as it is taught today. Salafism has inspired the Islamic violence which has inflicted one atrocity after another on civilized societies across the globe. It will continue to do so if we do not attack it on many different levels.

Terrorism is only a symptom of Islamism. Islamism is an abscess which has affected the whole body of the Muslim world. However, the Islamic nation is not sick because of the abscess. Rather, the abscess exists because the Islamic nation is sick. If we do not understand this distinction, we will treat the symptom and not the disease. More abscesses will appear and they will become more severe. As tragic as the events were on 9/11, they pale in comparison to what would happen should Islamic terrorists detonate a nuclear weapon or engage in biological warfare.

It would be bad enough if the world suffered merely from Islamic terror, but the human rights catastrophe spawned by Sharia law is a stain upon us all. Sharia has created, in Islamic societies, a horrific environment of abuse and oppression. Non-Muslims are second-class citizens; women are beaten and stoned to death for having sexual relations as they wish; gays hang from the gallows simply because of their orientation. Young Muslims, too, see their lives and futures destroyed by Islamist indoctrination. In the past, many in the West took refuge in the false impression that Sharia is a problem strictly in Middle Eastern nations. But that is not the case. Muslims in the West seek even now to implement Sharia and overturn the freedoms of modern, democratic nations. We see this in Iraq today, and it can happen in any civilized nation once Islamists have reached critical mass. We saw the society that Islamists envisioned in the form of the Taliban regime, and we see elements of it today in Saudi Arabia. If we do not act, it can reach Europe or America. While Islamism is in one sense like cancer, in another sense it resembles the bird flu. Like a cancer, it will grow worse if you ignore it inside your body; like the bird flu, if you ignore it in another part of the world, it will be transmitted to you.

If we do not understand the process behind Islamic terrorism we cannot defeat it. We must be objective and scientific, even if it hurts our pride or if we fear to offend people. Political correctness interferes with logical, objective threat assessments. We must stop finding unsupportable, external justifications for terror. Religious sensitivity to Muslims is actually harmful to Muslim and non-Muslim alike – without constructive criticism of Salafi Islam, Muslims will never feel the need to reform or reinterpret violent doctrine. Excessive hesitancy to expose the violent edicts of Sharia is impeding the process of reformation within then Islamic world. This reformation is needed today more than ever, no less than it was necessary for other faiths at various stages in their history.

Islamic terrorism is a phenomenon with a clear pattern. Understanding this pattern and addressing every step of the Islamization process is fundamental to defeating Jihadism in the long run. Working only at the terrorism level may temporary relieve the painful symptoms of Islamism, but will not cure the disease itself.

Muslims have an important role in the war on Islamism. They must stand clearly against terrorists (not just against *terrorism*) and also against the violent teaching that pervades mainstream Islamic books. Islam can and must be reformed in order to inoculate young Muslims against violent indoctrination. As for myself, my own thoughts and actions have been geared not to destroying Islam, but to saving Islam. My goal is, and has always been, to save the next generation of young Muslims – and society in general – from the catastrophe of Islamism.

Appendices

A Poem by Dr. Maha Hamid

Finding excuses and justification for Islamism Terrorism has become a fashion these days. We wish to avoid confronting the real problem of Salafism and to blame everyone but the Islamists. This has lead many to claim that terrorism is an understandable outcome of Muslim rage at perceived mistreatment by non-Muslims. My wife, Dr. Maha Hamid has written a poem in response to these excuses.

Who should be angry?

Should it be Muslims who kill innocents everywhere in the name of God?

Or should it be...

> *...the Christians who saw their churches burnt by Muslims in Iraq and elsewhere?*

> *...the Jews who see their kids die in Pizza Parlors?*

> *...the Buddhists who saw their ancient statues of Bhudda destroyed by Taliban?*

> *...the Hindus who witnessed their most holy temple burnt to the ground at the hands of Muslims?*

> *...the Sikh, when Muslims burnt one of their gurus alive as he preached a message of peace and love?*

Who should be angry?

> *The Muslims who bless such evil terrorism by their deafening silence against it?*

Or should it be...

> *...the Russians who lost their kids in the Beslan school massacre?*

…the Americans who lost thousands of innocent people on September 11th

…the British families whose loved ones were murdered on July 7 by UK-born Muslims?

…the Spanish, who lost hundreds of citizens when Muslims blew up their trains?

…the Australians who lost their sons and daughters when jihadists destroyed the Bali nightclubs?

Who should be angry?

The Muslims who never denounced Bin Laden strongly?

Or should it be…

…the child who lost his mum when jihadists attacked?

…the daughter who lost her father from jihadist evil?

…the mother who lost her kids in cowardly acts of terror?

…the grandmother who lost her grand kids Islamist atrocities?

Who should be angry?

Muslims who produced the terrorism by preaching hate in mosques?

Or should it be…

…the writer who lost his hand in a terrorist explosion?

…the young boy who lost his legs and cannot play football anymore?

…the musician who lost his fingers and can no longer play?

….the teenager who got her face mutilated by the fire of Islamic terrorism?

Who should be angry?

Muslims who celebrated 9/11, mutilated dead bodies, or beheaded hostages on videotape?

Or should it be…

….the whole world who suffers from Islamic terror every day?

Who should be angry?

— Maha Hamid

The Amman Statement

The Amman Statment

"In the Name of Allah, the Compassionate, the Merciful

Peace and Blessings be upon our master Muhammad and his Family

"O mankind! Be careful of your duty to your Lord Who created you

from a single soul…" (Al-Nisa', 4:1)

Statement issued by the International Islamic Conference held in Amman, the Hashemite Kingdom of Jordan, under the title:

"True Islam and its Role in Modern Society"

27-29 I Jumada 1426 H./4-6 Tammuz (July) 2005 CE.

In accordance with the fatwas issued by the Honorable and Respectable Grand Imam Shaykh al-Azhar, the Grand Ayatollah Al-Sayyid Ali Al-Sistani, the Honorable and Respectable Grand Mufti of Egypt, the Honorable and Respectable Shi'i clerics (both Ja'fari and Zaidi), the Honorable and Respectable Grand Mufti of the Sultanate of Oman, the Islamic Fiqh Academy in the Kingdom of Saudi Arabia, the Grand Council for Religious Affairs of Turkey, the Honorable and Respectable Grand Mufti of the Hashemite Kingdom of Jordan and the Respectable Members of its National Fatwa Committee, and the Honorable and Respectable Shaykh Dr. Yusuf Al-Qaradawi; And in accordance with what was mentioned in the speech of His Hashemite Majesty King Abdullah II bin Al-Hussein, King of the Hashemite Kingdom of Jordan during the opening session of our conference;

And in accordance with our own knowledge in sincerity to Allah the Bounteous;

And in accordance with what was presented in this our conference by way of research papers and studies, and by way of the discussions that transpired in it;

We, the undersigned, hereby express our approval and affirmation of what appears below:

Whosoever is an adherent of one of the four Sunni Schools of Jurisprudence (Hanafi, Maliki, Shafi'i and Hanbali), the Ja'fari (Shi'i) School of Jurisprudence, the Zaydi School of Jurisprudence, the Ibadi School of Jurisprudence, or the Thahiri School of Jurisprudence is a Muslim. Declaring that person an apostate is impossible. Verily his (or her) blood, honor, and property are sacrosanct. Moreover, in accordance with what appeared in the fatwa of the Honorable and Respectable Shaykh al-Azhar, it is not possible to declare whosoever subscribes to the Ash'ari creed or whoever practices true Sufism an apostate. Likewise, it is not possible to declare whosoever subscribes to true Salafi thought an apostate. Equally, it is not possible to declare as apostates any group of Muslims who believes in Allah the Mighty and Sublime and His Messenger (may Peace and Blessings be upon him) and the pillars of faith, and respects the pillars of Islam and does not deny any "Maloom Mina Al-Din Bil-Darura" - necessary article of religion.

There exists more in common between the various Schools of Jurisprudence than there is difference. The adherents to the eight Schools of Jurisprudence are in agreement as regards the basic Islamic principles. All believe in Allah the Mighty and Sublime, the One and the Unique; that the Noble Qur'an is the Revealed Word of Allah; and that our master Muhammad, may Blessings and Peace be upon him, is a Prophet and Messenger unto all mankind. All are in agreement about the five pillars of Islam: the two testaments of faith (shahadatayn), the ritual prayer (salat), almsgiving (zakat), fasting in the month of Ramadan (sawm), and the Hajj to the Sacred House of Allah. All are also in agreement about the foundations of belief: belief in Allah, His Angels, His Scriptures, His Messengers, and in the Day of Judgement, in Divine providence—good and evil. Disagreement between the 'ulama' is only with respect to the ancillary branches of religion (furu') and not the principles and fundamentals (usul). Disagreement with respect to the ancillary branches of religion (furu') is a mercy. Long ago it was said that variance in opinion among 'ulama' "is a good affair".

Acknowledgement of the Schools of Jurisprudence within Islam means adhering to a fundamental methodology in the issuance of fatwas. No one may issue a fatwa without the requisite personal qualifications which each School of Jurisprudence defines. No one may issue a fatwa without adhering to the methodology of the Schools of Jurisprudence. No one may claim to do absolute Ijtihad and create a new School of Jurisprudence or to issue unacceptable fatwas that take Muslims out of the principles and certainties of the Shari'ah and what has been established in respect to its Schools of Jurisprudence.

The essence of the Amman Message, which was issued on the Blessed Night of Power in the year 1425 H. and which was read aloud in Masjid al-Hashimiyyin, is adherence to the Schools of Jurisprudence and their fundamental methodology. Acknowledging the Schools of Jurisprudence and affirming discussion and engagement between them ensures fairness, moderation, mutual forgiveness, compassion, and engaging in dialogue with others. We call for casting aside disagreement between Muslims and unifying their words and stances; reaffirming their mutual respect for each other; fortifying mutual affinity among their peoples and states; strengthening the ties of brotherhood which unite them in the mutual love of Allah. And we call upon Muslims to not permit discord and outside interference between them.

Allah the Sublime says:

"The believers are naught else than brothers. Therefore make peace between your brethren and observe your duty to Allah that haply ye may obtain mercy." (Al-Hujurat, 49:10)

PRAISE BE TO ALLAH ALONE.

- Doesn't mention any terrorist by name

- Doesn't mention killing non-Muslims, only not allowed to kill Muslims

- Does allow killing Muslims who deny "necessary articles"

FBI Hate Crime Statistics

Table 1
Incidents, Offenses, Victims, and Known Offenders
by Bias Motivation, 2006

Bias motivation	Incidents	Offenses	Victims [1]	Known offenders [2]
Total	7,722	9,080	9,652	7,330
Single-Bias Incidents	7,720	9,076	9,642	7,324
Race:	4,000	4,737	5,020	3,957
Anti-White	890	1,008	1,054	1,074
Anti-Black	2,640	3,136	3,332	2,437
Anti-American Indian/Alaskan Native	60	72	75	72
Anti-Asian/Pacific Islander	181	230	239	181
Anti-Multiple Races, Group	229	291	320	193
Religion:	1,462	1,597	1,750	705
Anti-Jewish	967	1,027	1,144	362
Anti-Catholic	76	81	86	44
Anti-Protestant	59	62	65	35
Anti-Islamic	156	191	208	147
Anti-Other Religion	124	140	147	63
Anti-Multiple Religions, Group	73	88	92	49
Anti-Atheism/Agnosticism/etc.	7	8	8	5
Sexual Orientation:	1,195	1,415	1,472	1,380
Anti-Male Homosexual	747	881	913	914
Anti-Female Homosexual	163	192	202	154
Anti-Homosexual	238	293	307	268
Anti-Heterosexual	26	28	29	26
Anti-Bisexual	21	21	21	18
Ethnicity/National Origin:	984	1,233	1,305	1,209
Anti-Hispanic	576	770	819	802
Anti-Other Ethnicity/National Origin	408	463	486	407
Disability:	79	94	95	73
Anti-Physical	17	20	21	17
Anti-Mental	62	74	74	56
Multiple-Bias Incidents [3]	2	4	10	6

[1] The term *victim* may refer to a person, business, institution, or society as a whole.
[2] The term *known offender* does not imply that the identity of the suspect is known, but only that an attribute of the suspect has been identified, which distinguishes him/her from an unknown offender.
[3] In a *multiple-bias incident*, two conditions must be met: (a) more than one offense type must occur in the incident and (b) at least two offense types must be motivated by different biases.

This table is available online at the FBI's website: http://www.fbi.gov/ucr/hc2006/table1.html